Simple
COLORING BOOK

THIS BOOK BELONGS TO

COLOR TEST

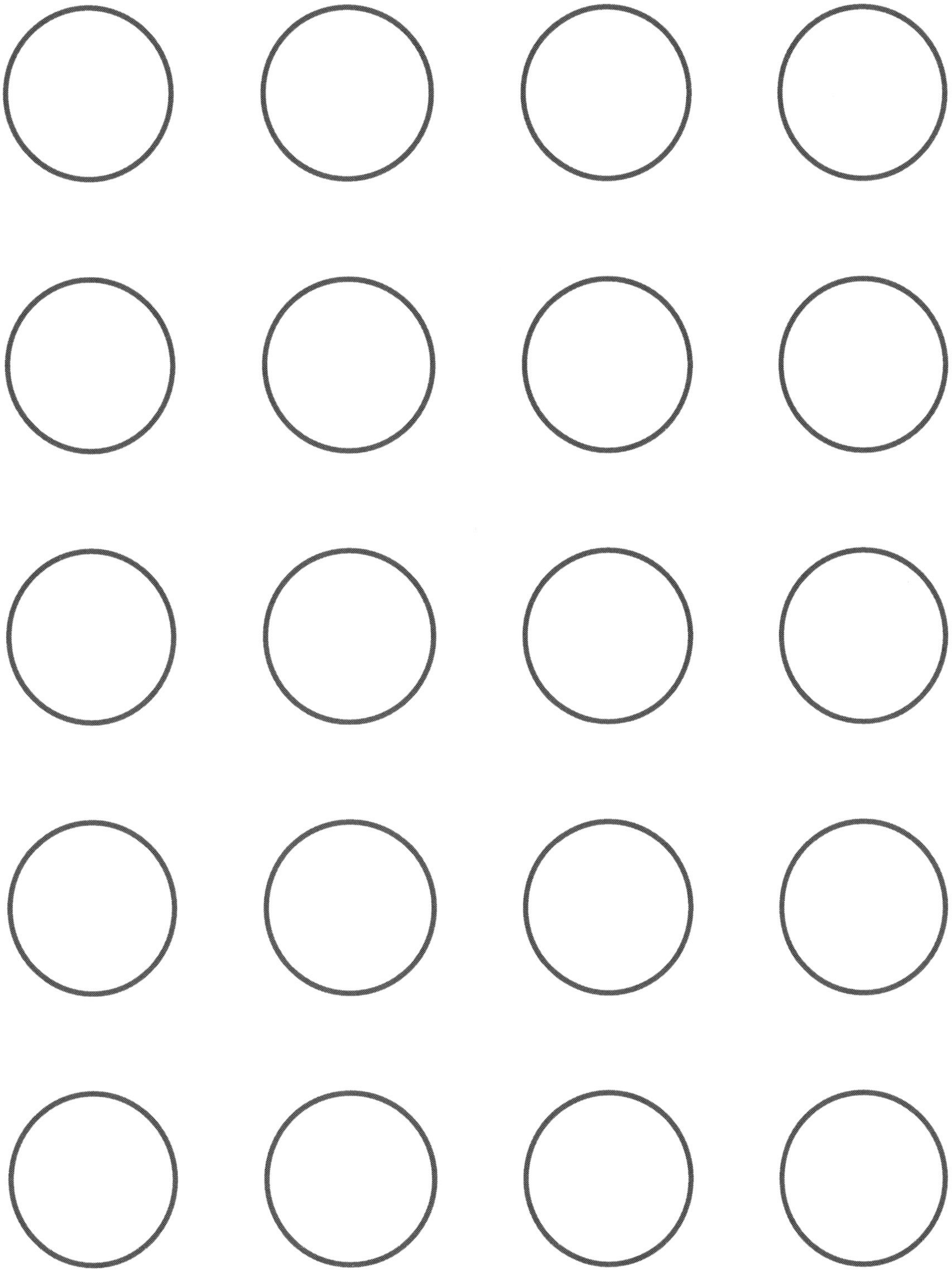

COLOR TEST

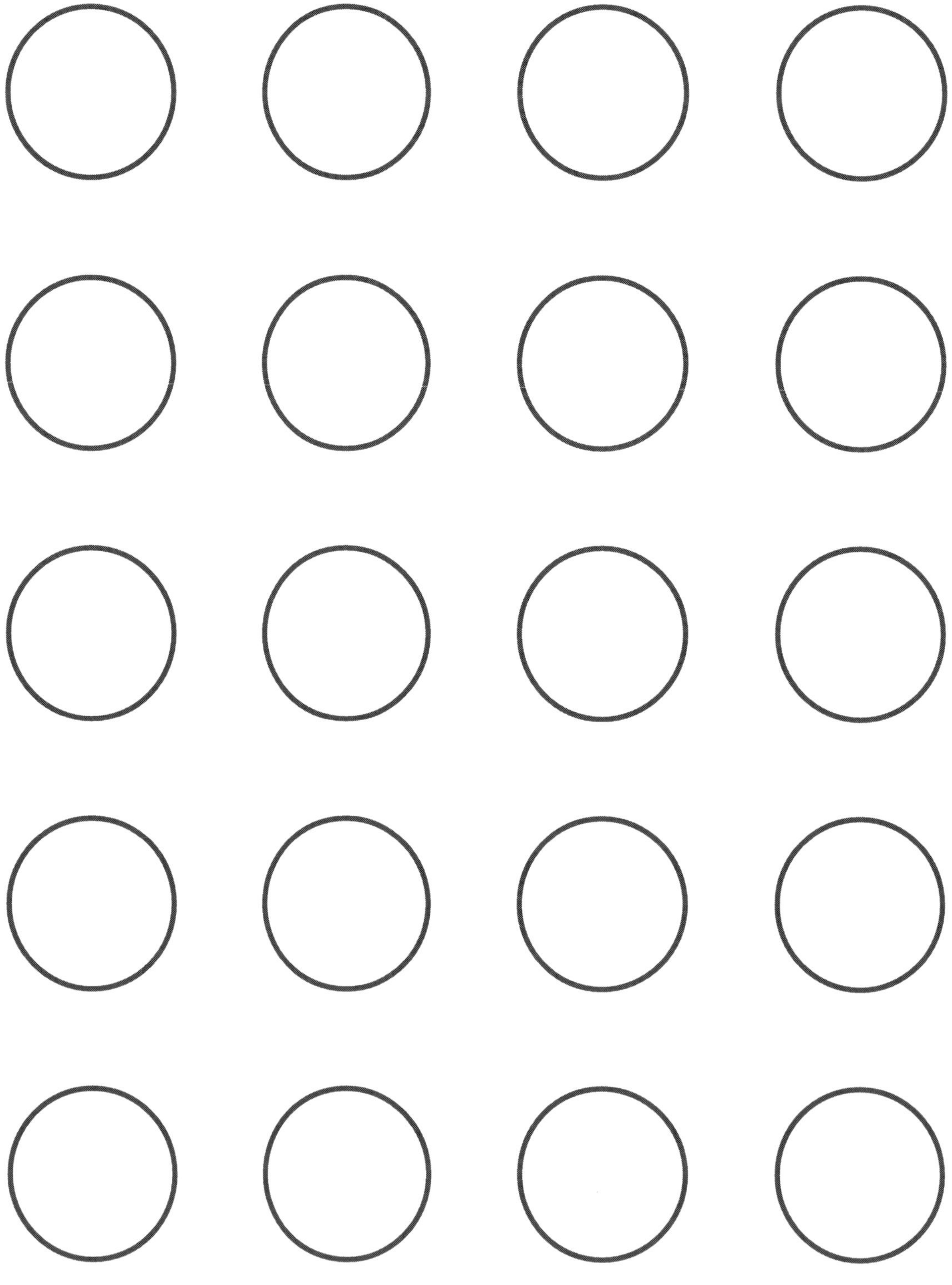

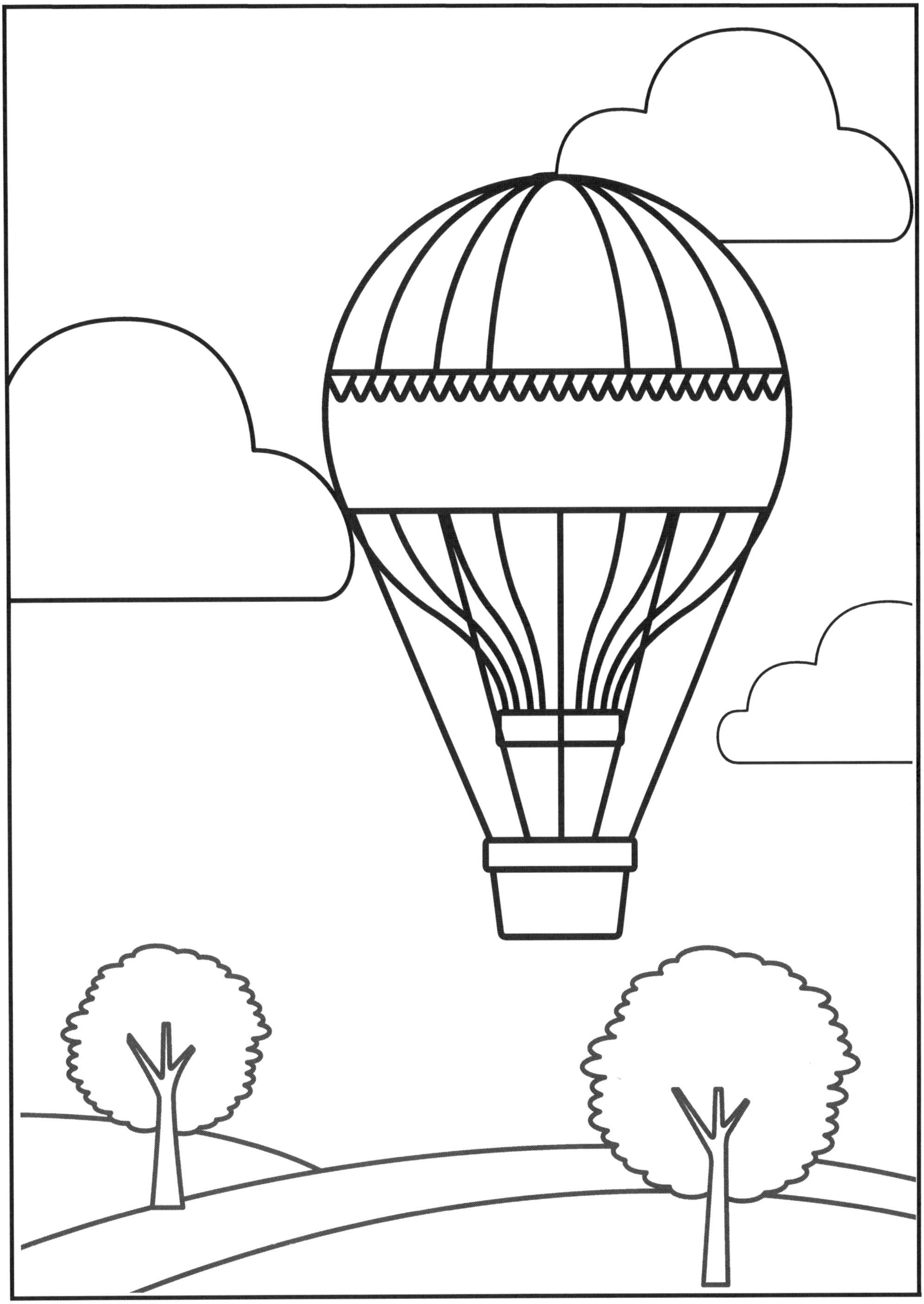

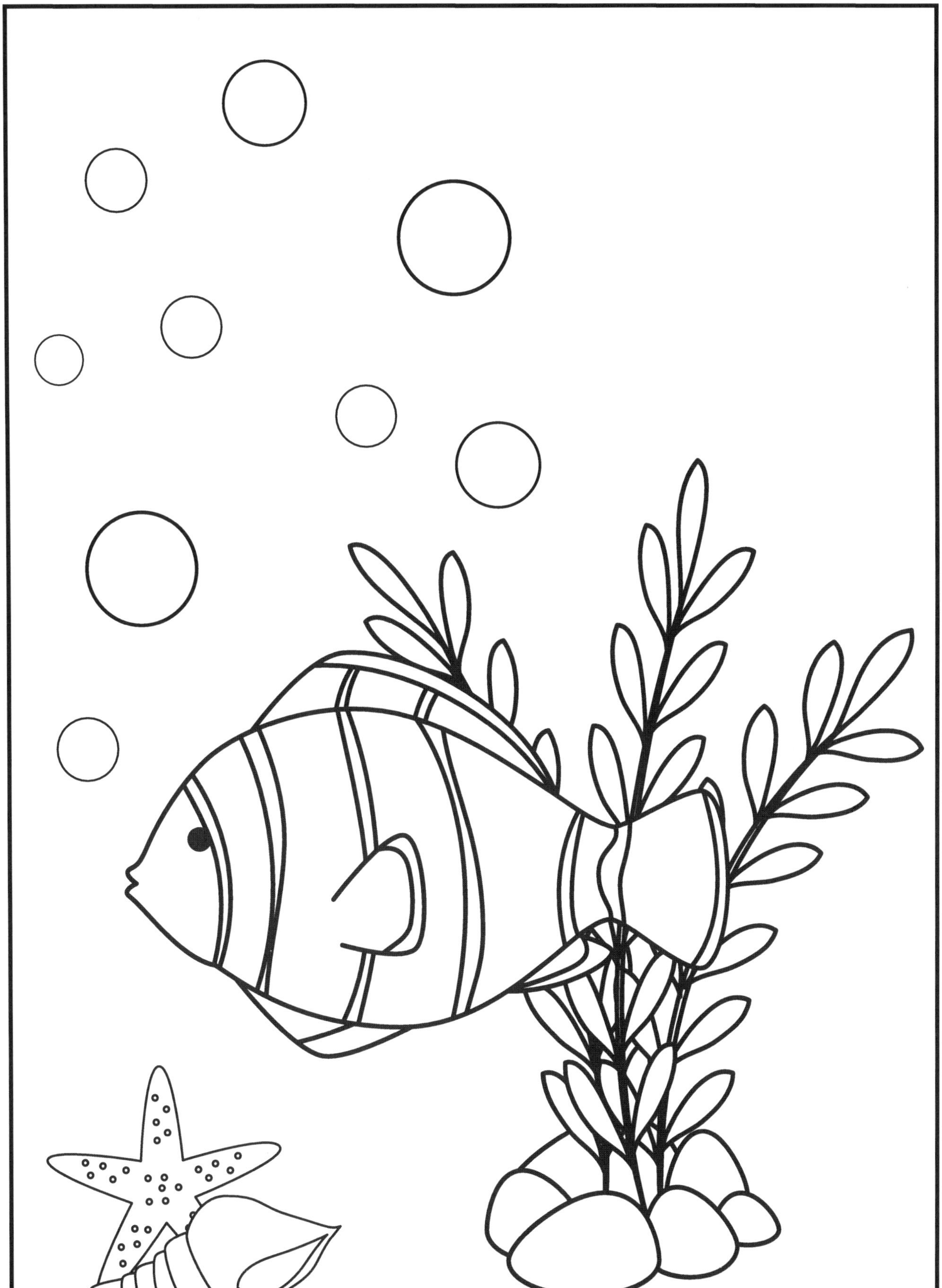

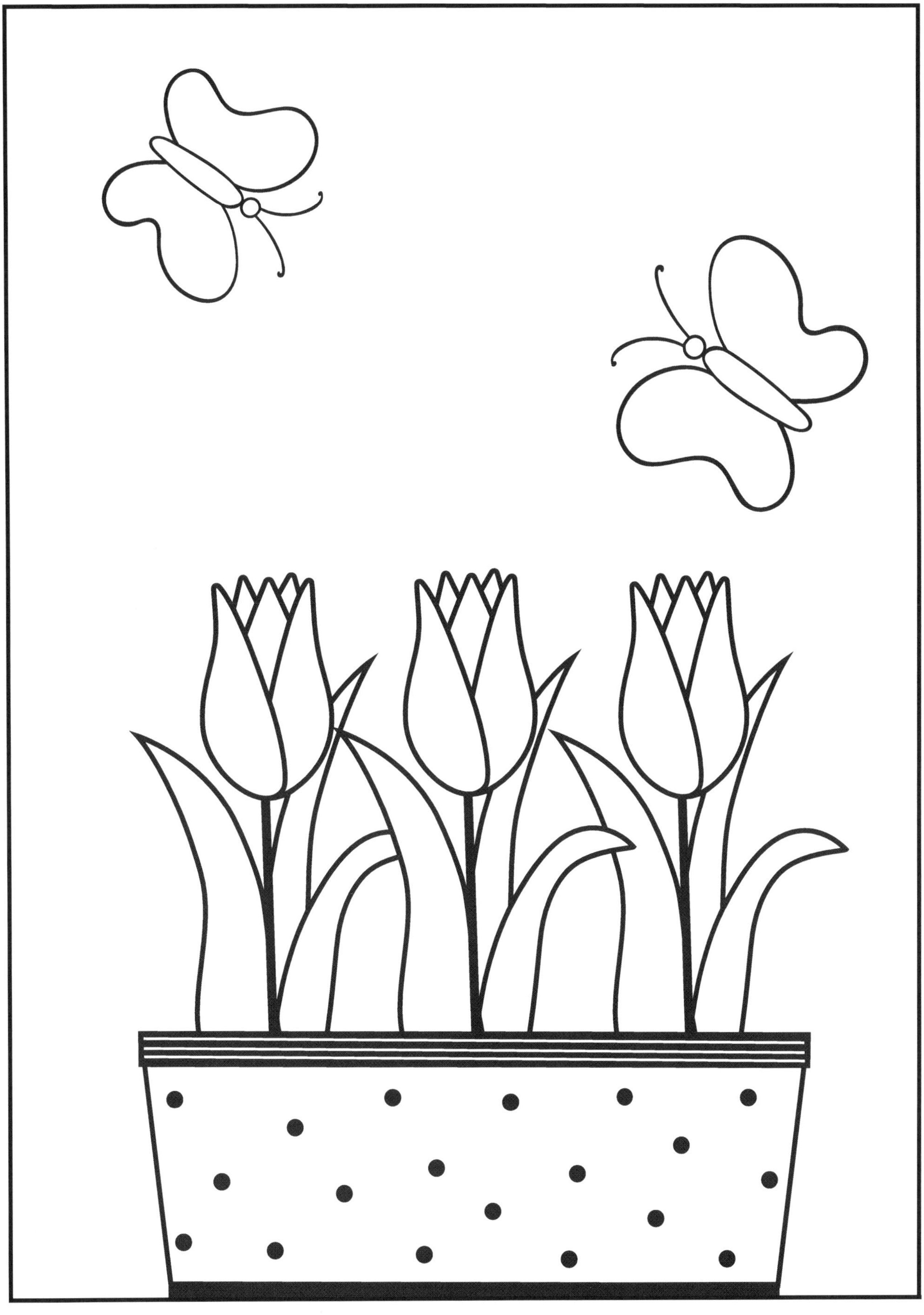

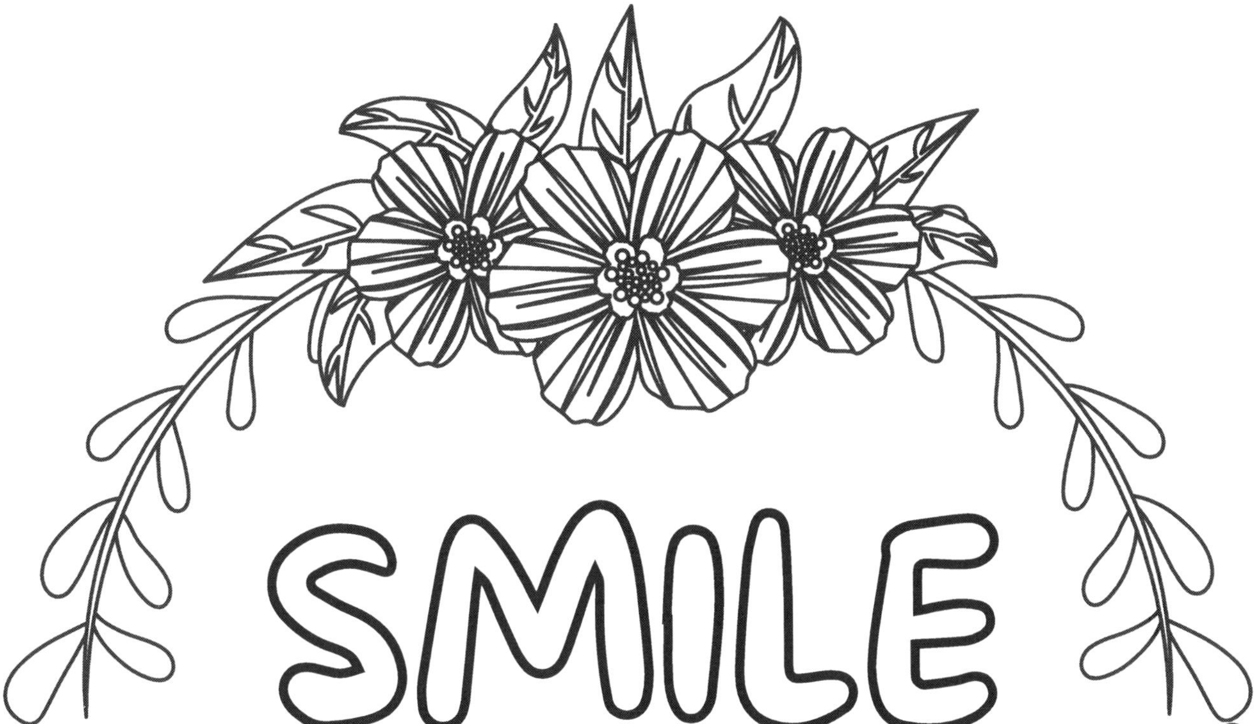
SMILE
EVERYDAY

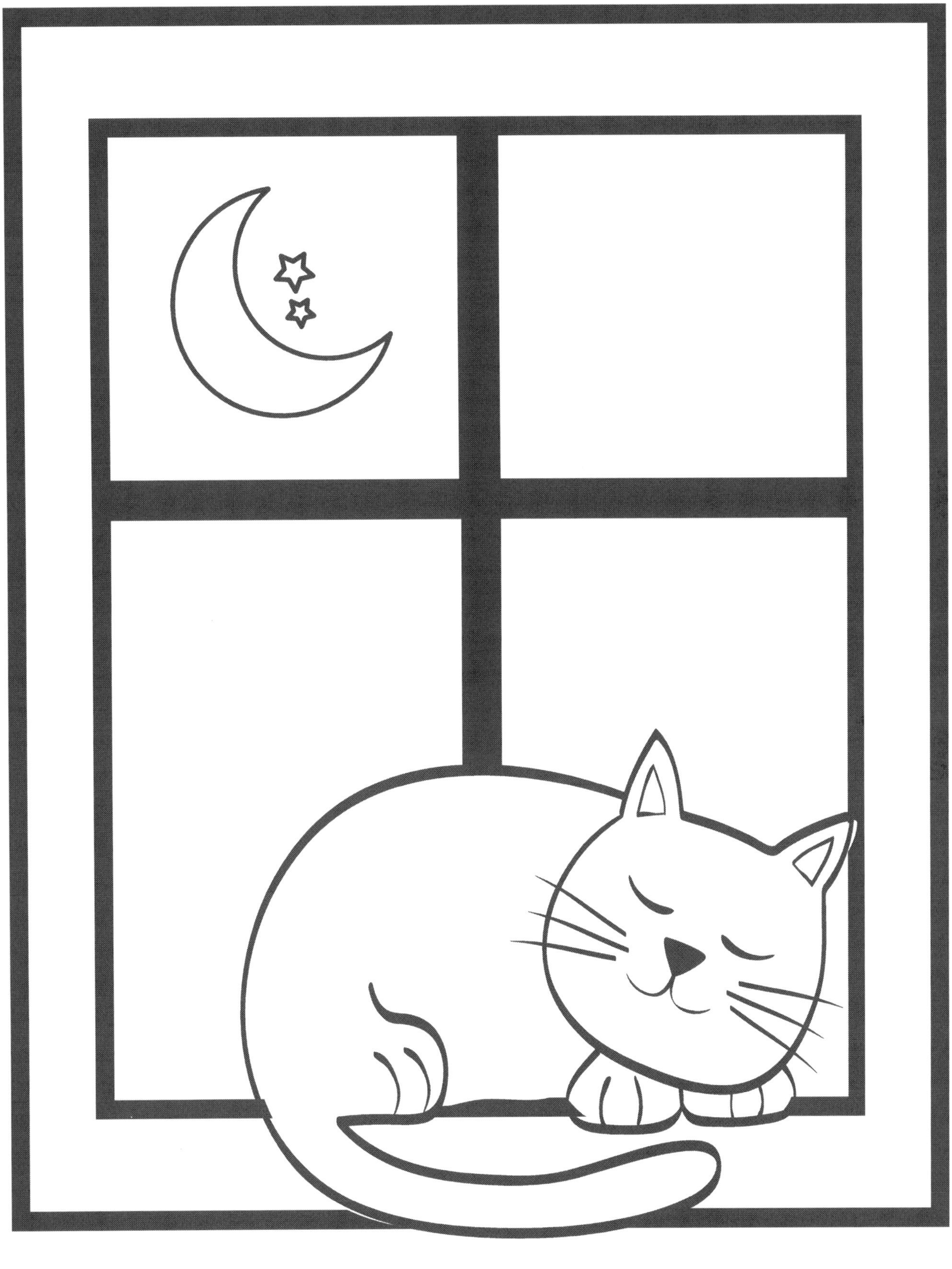

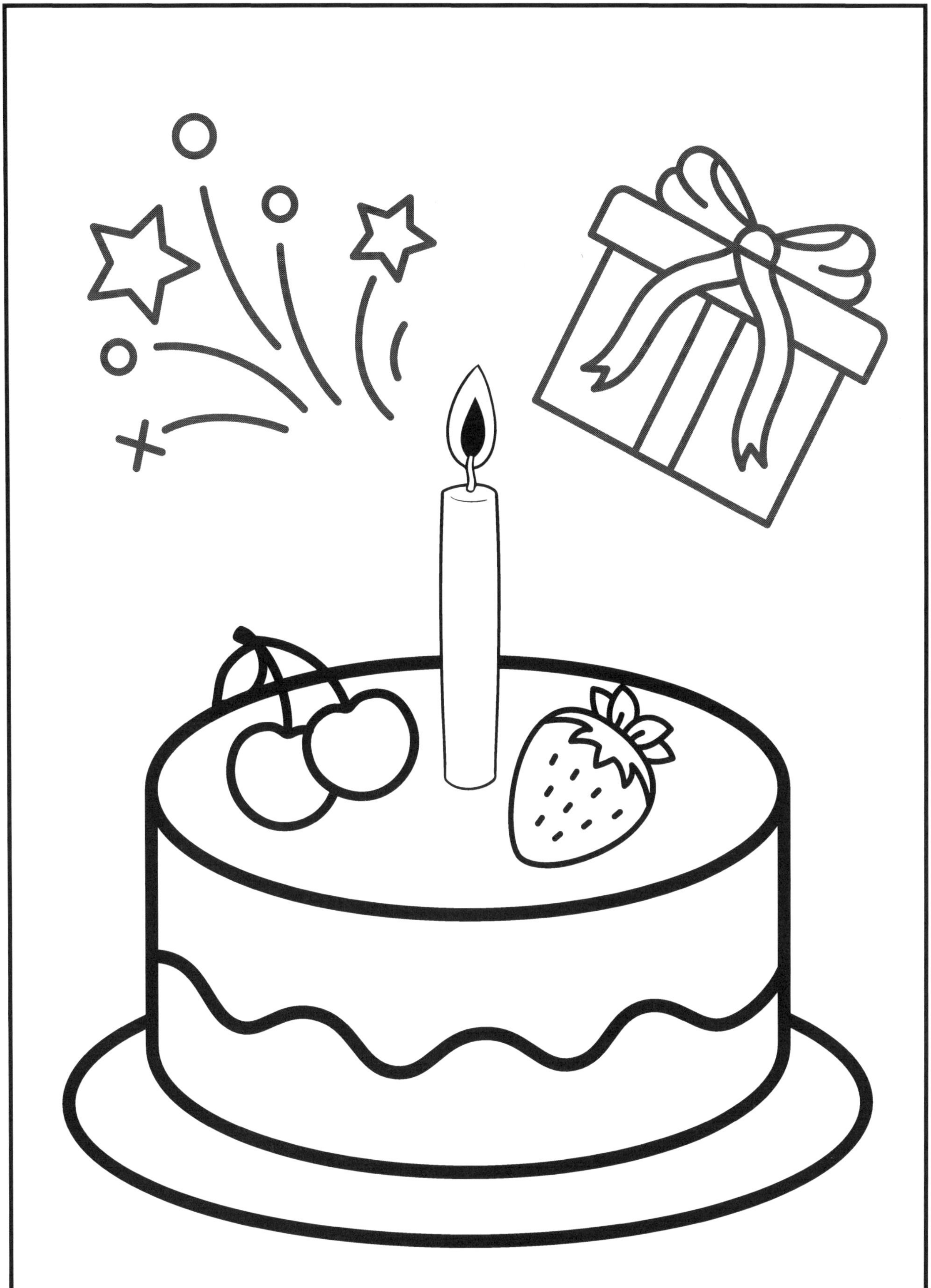

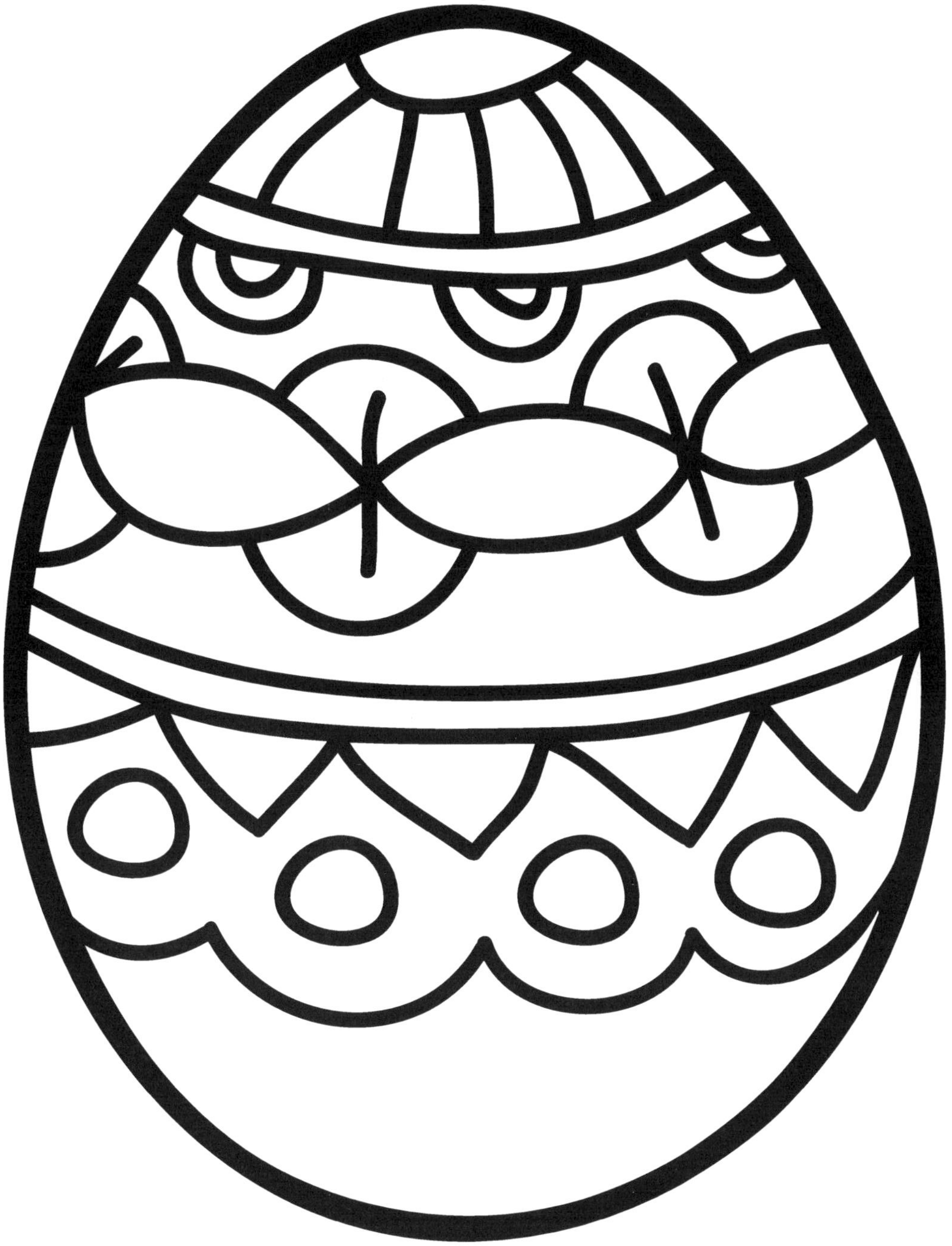

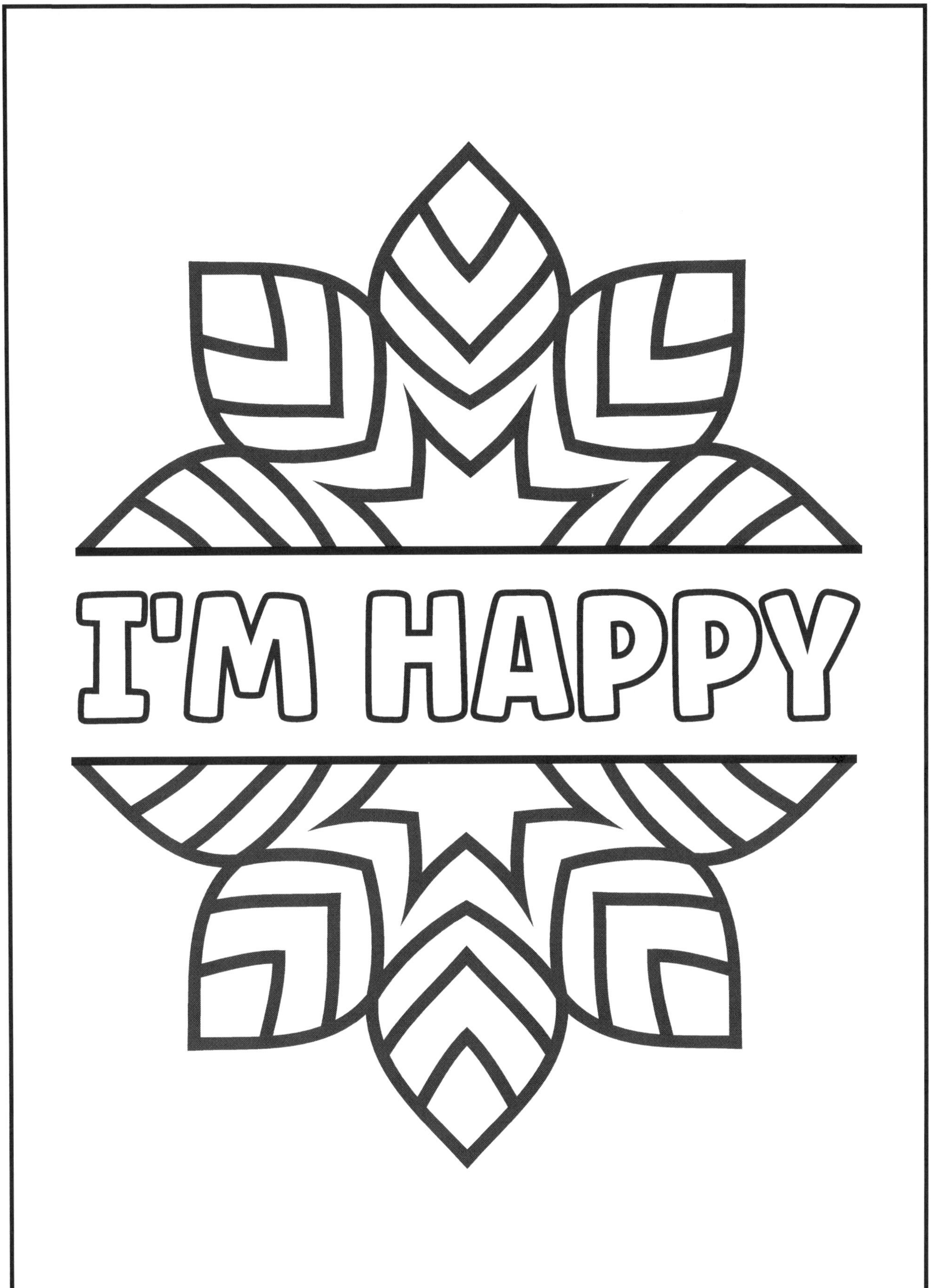
I'M HAPPY

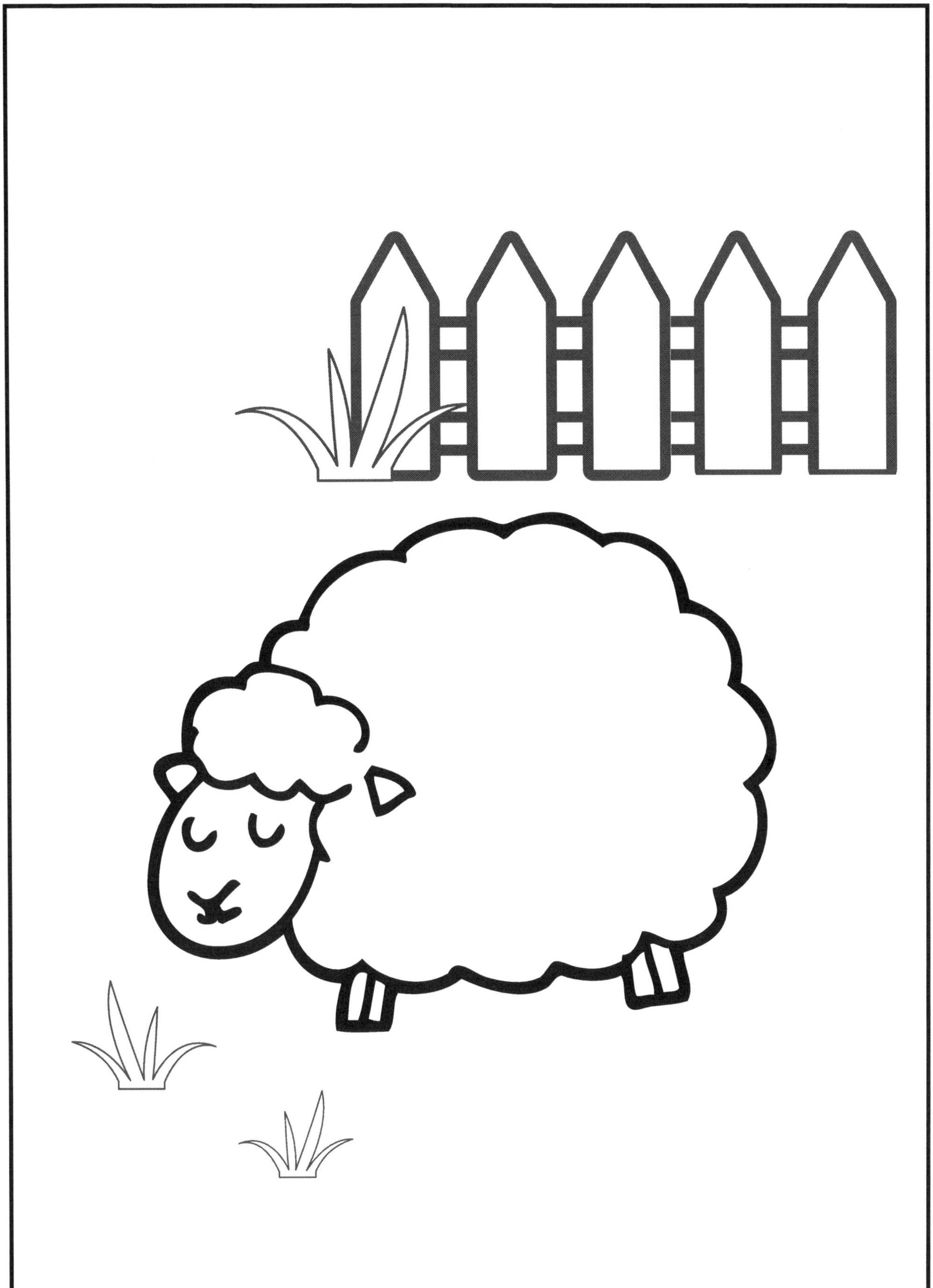

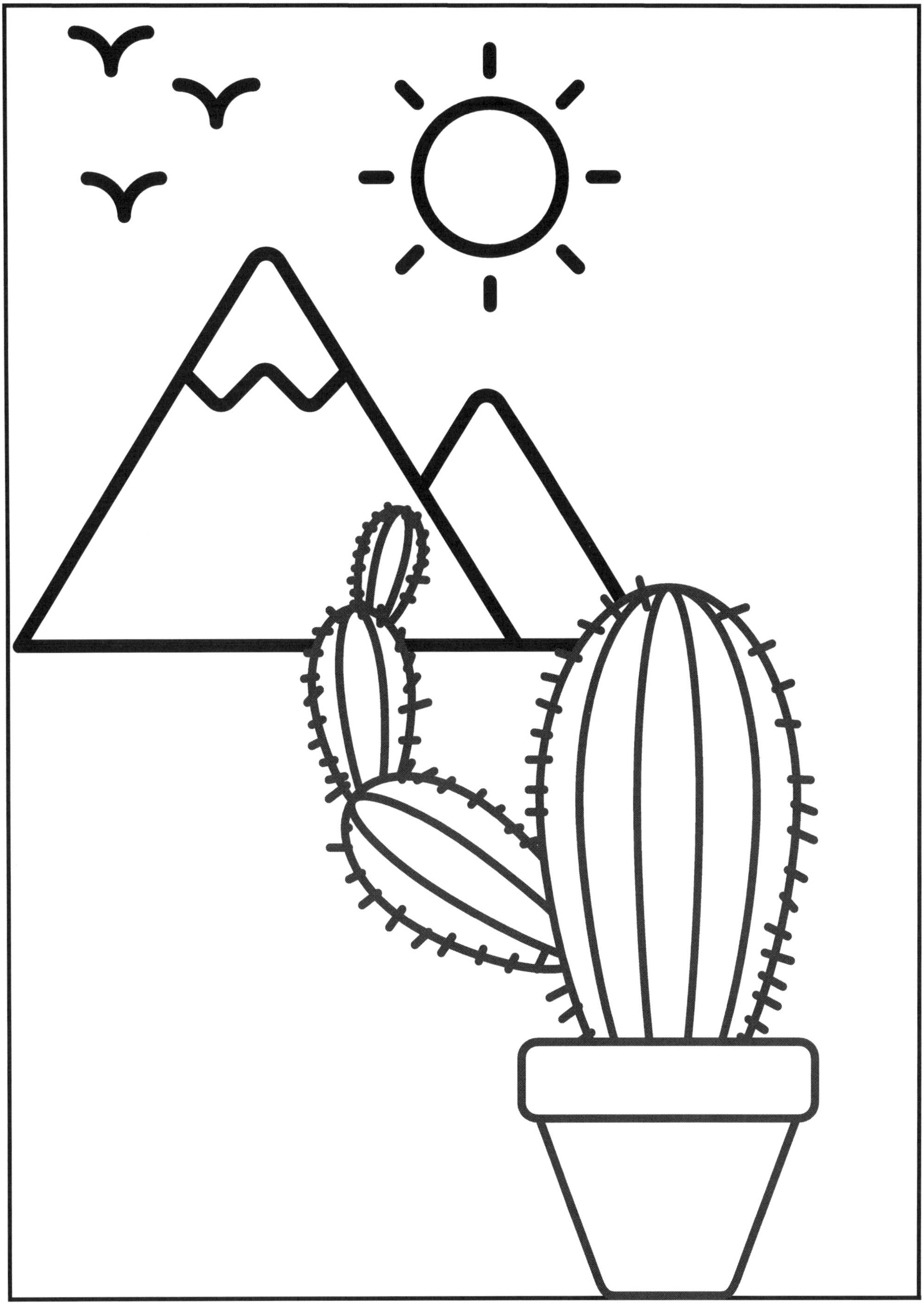

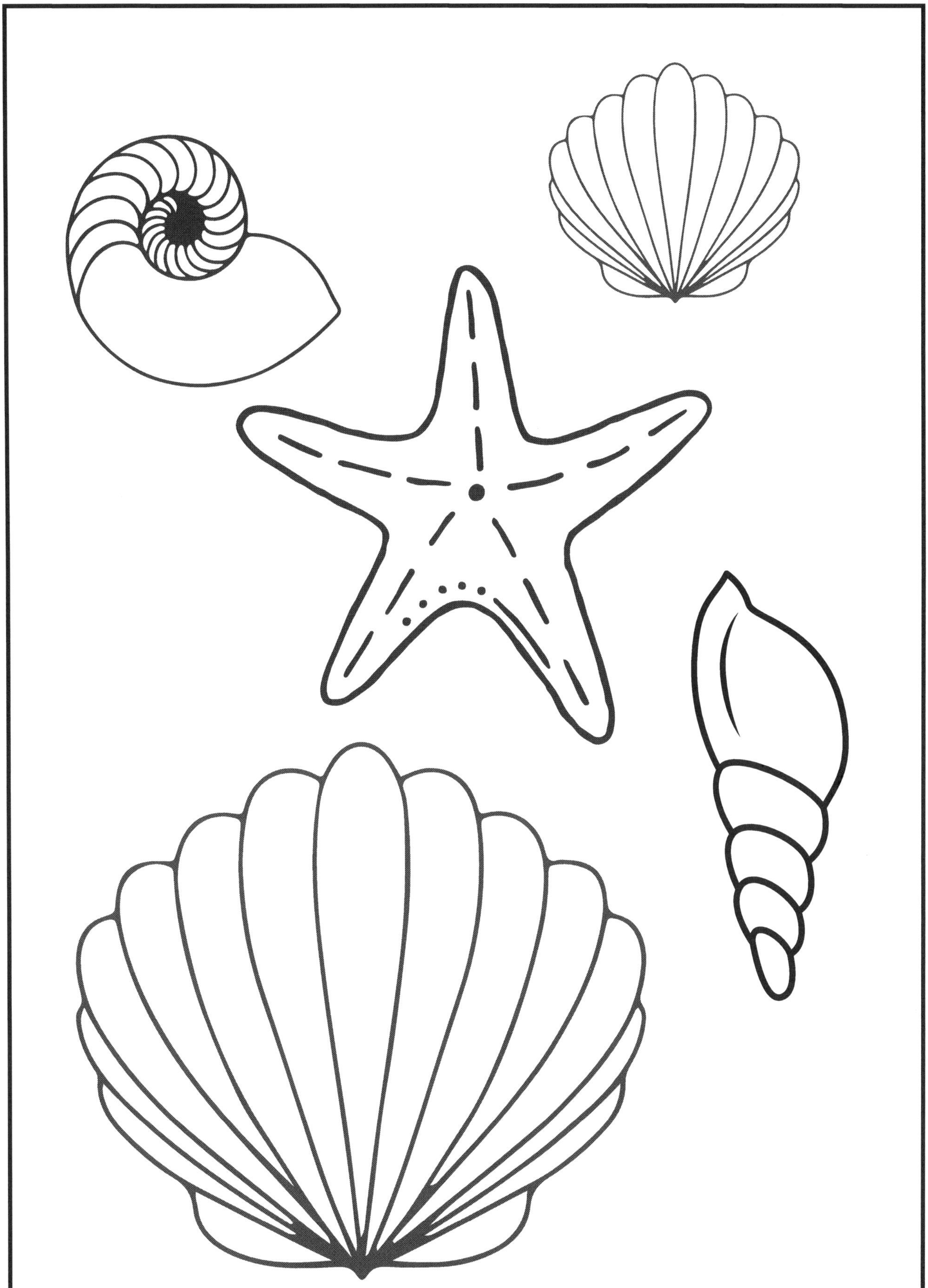

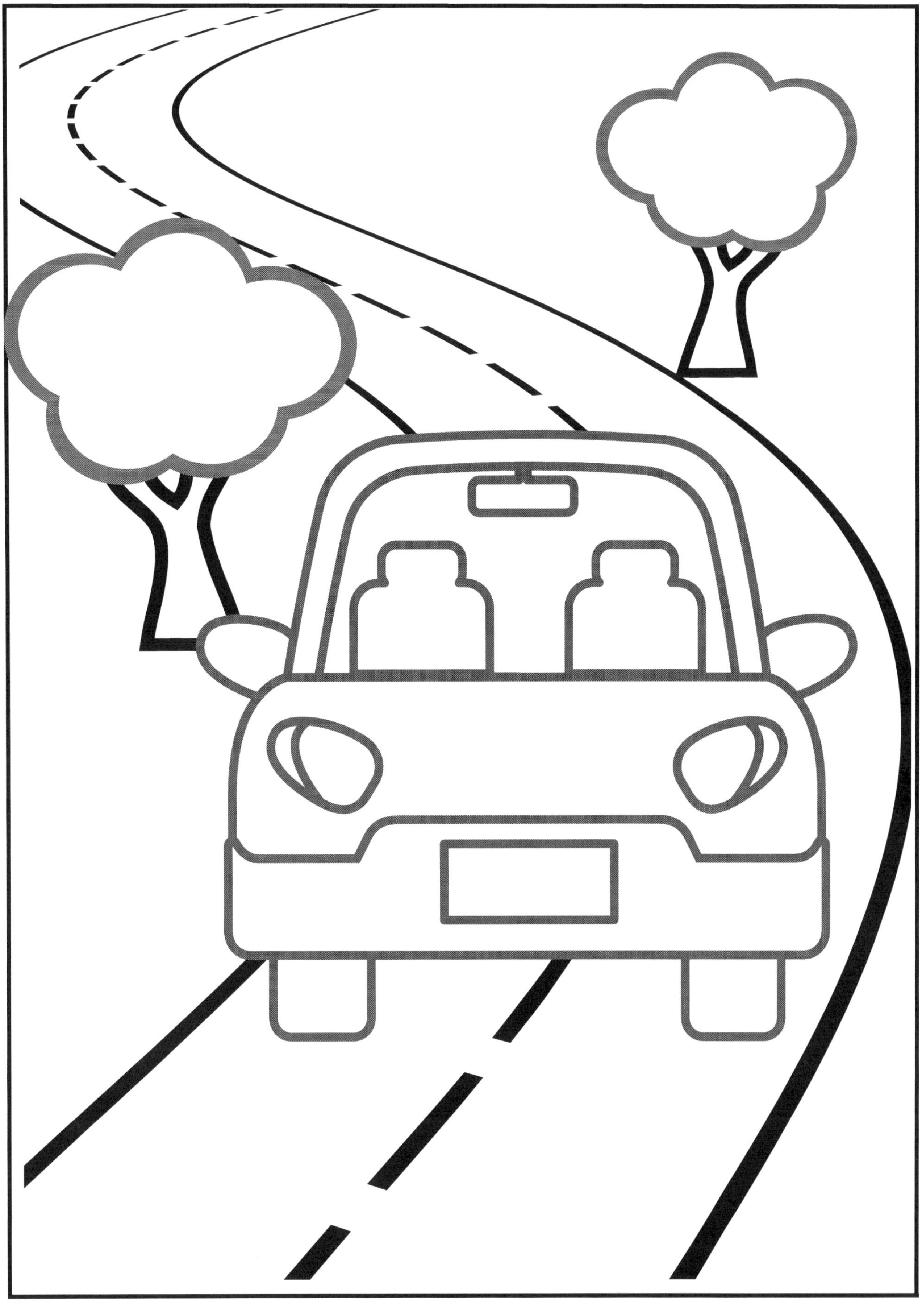

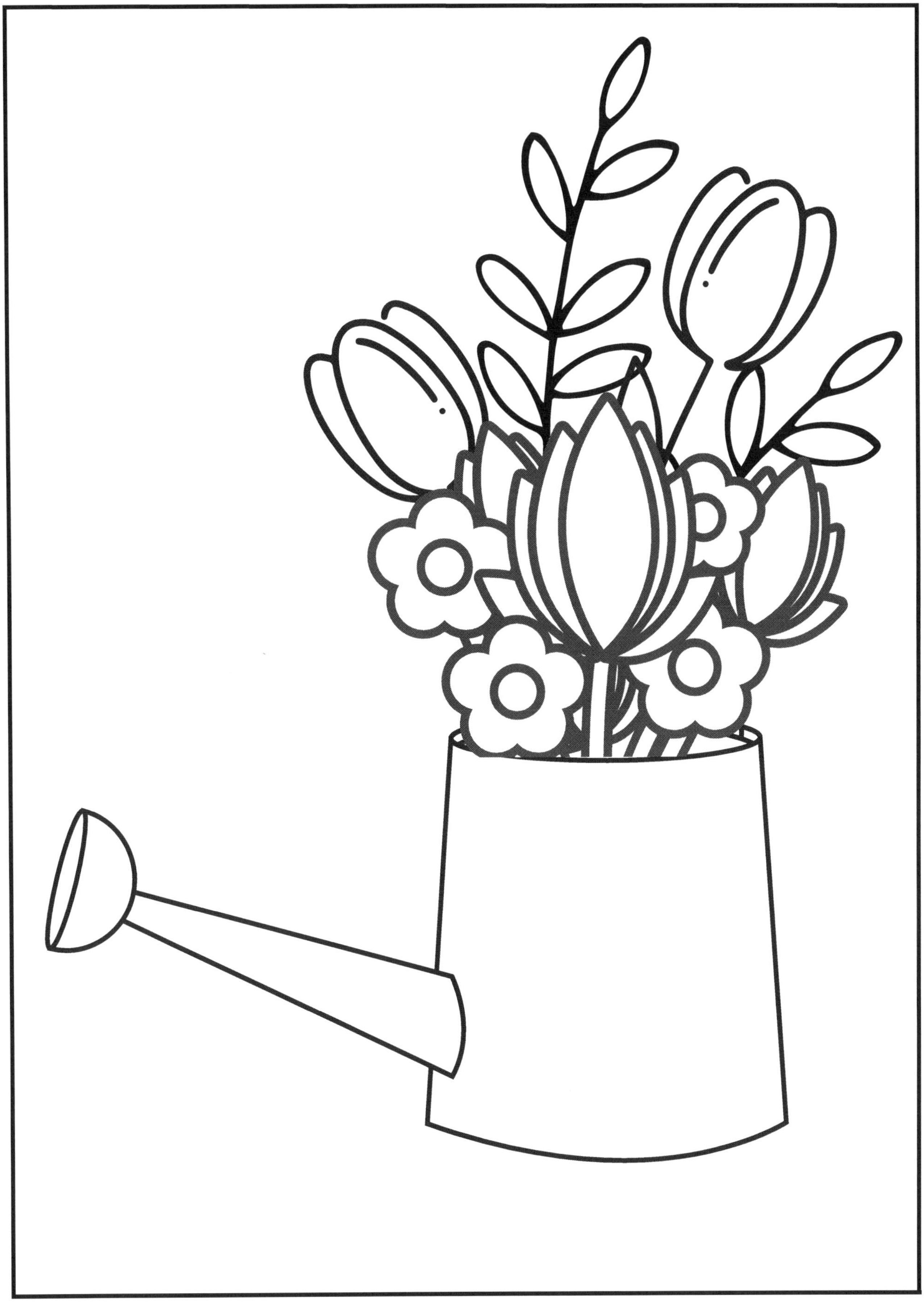

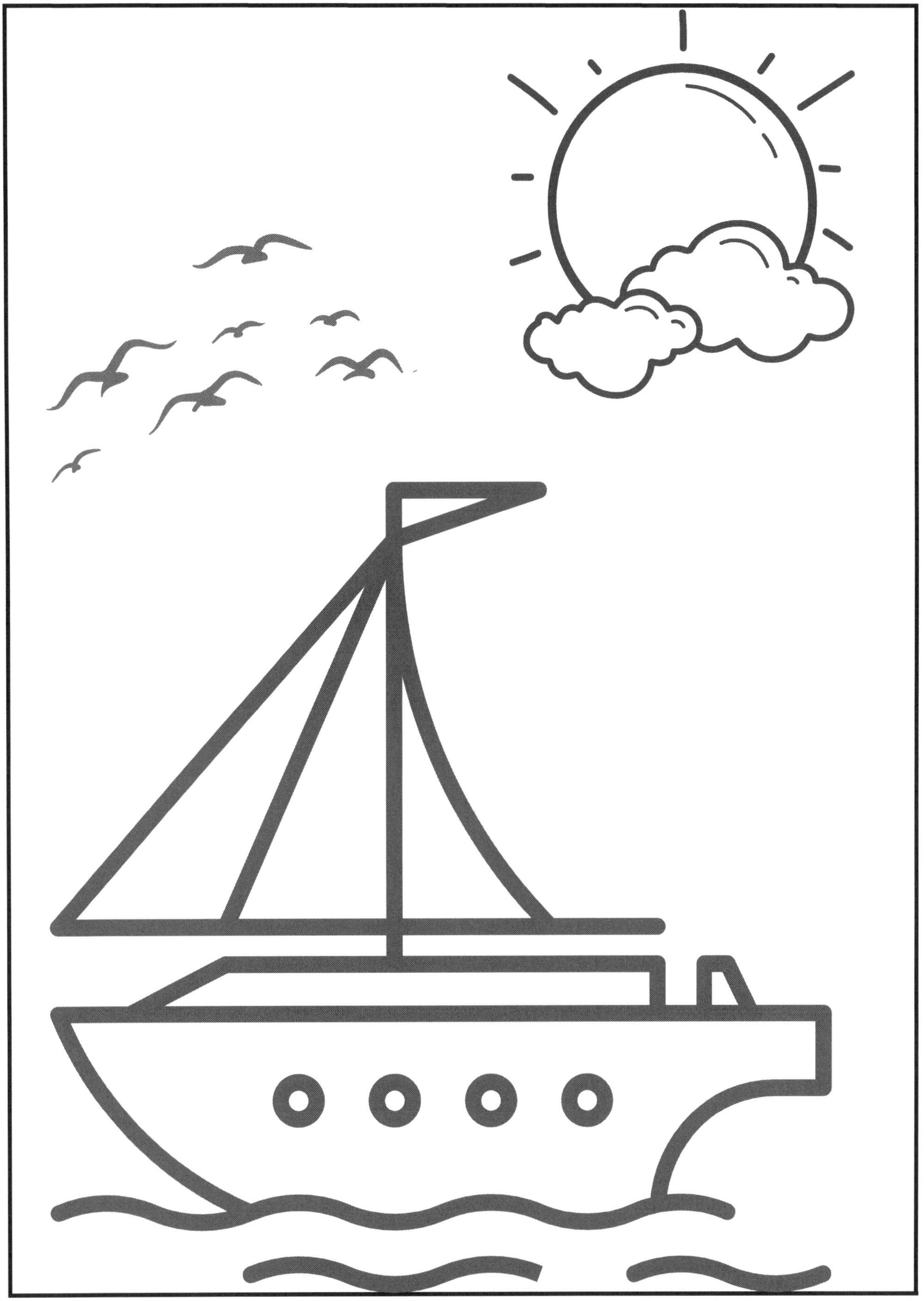

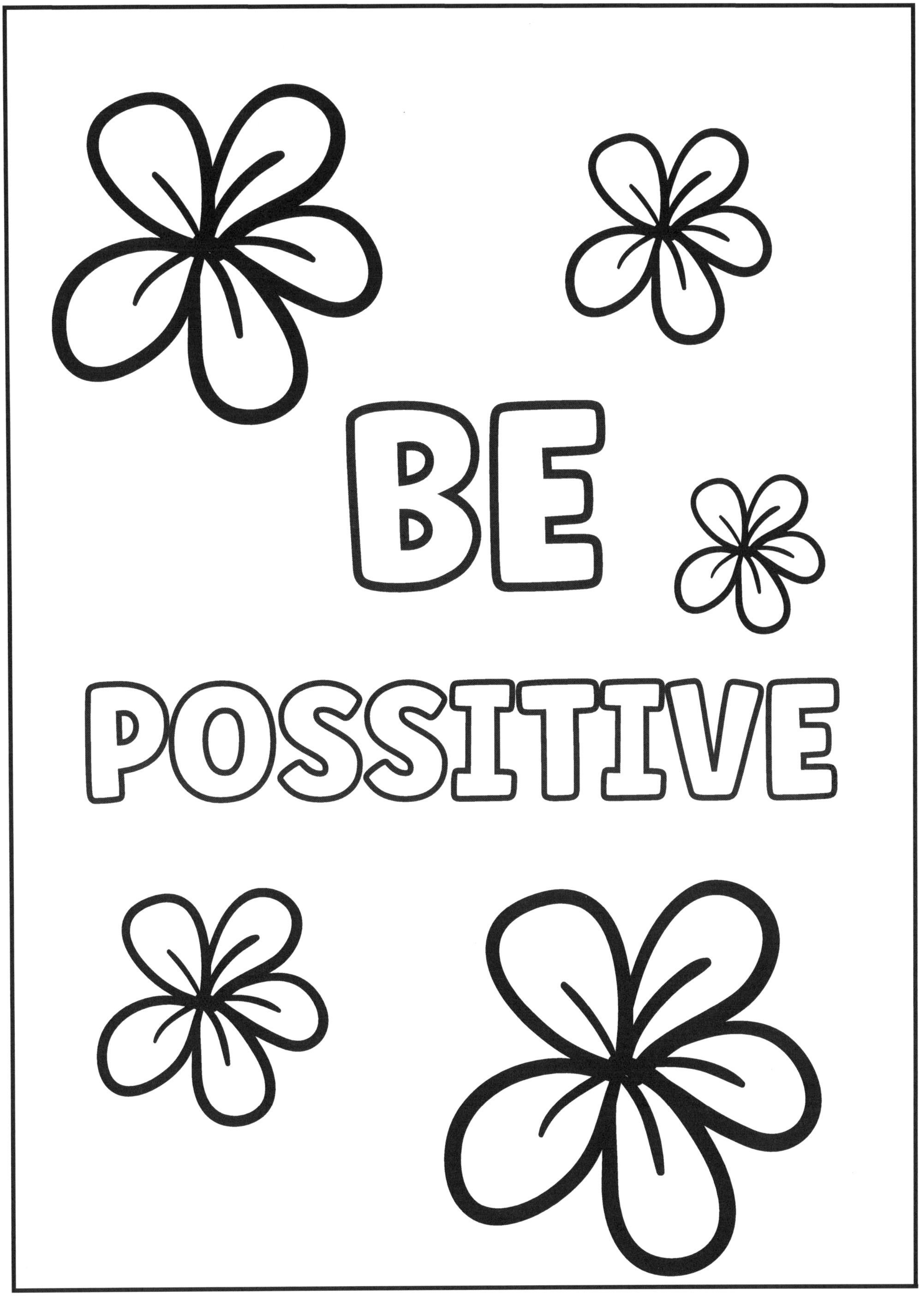
BE
POSSITIVE

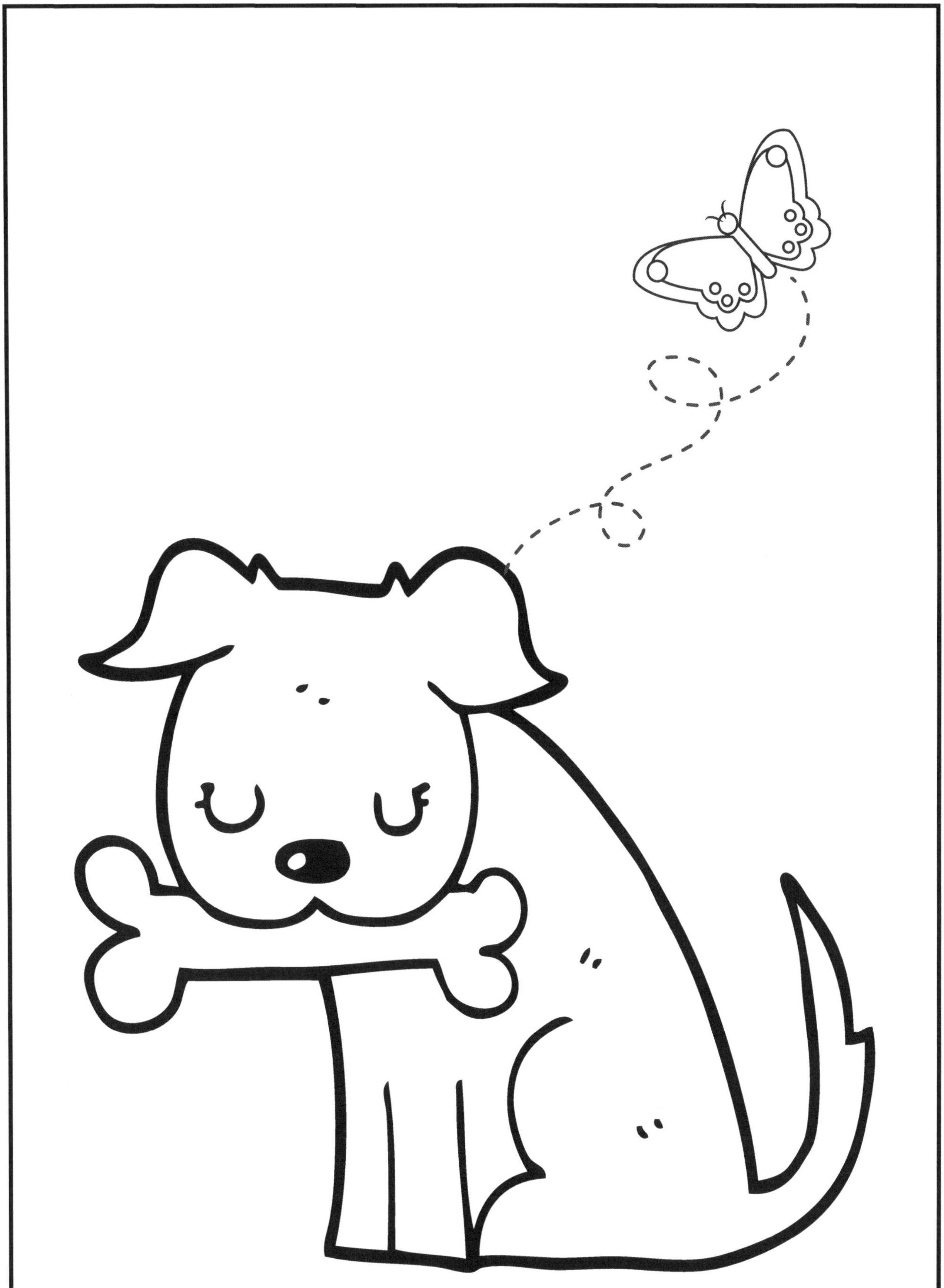

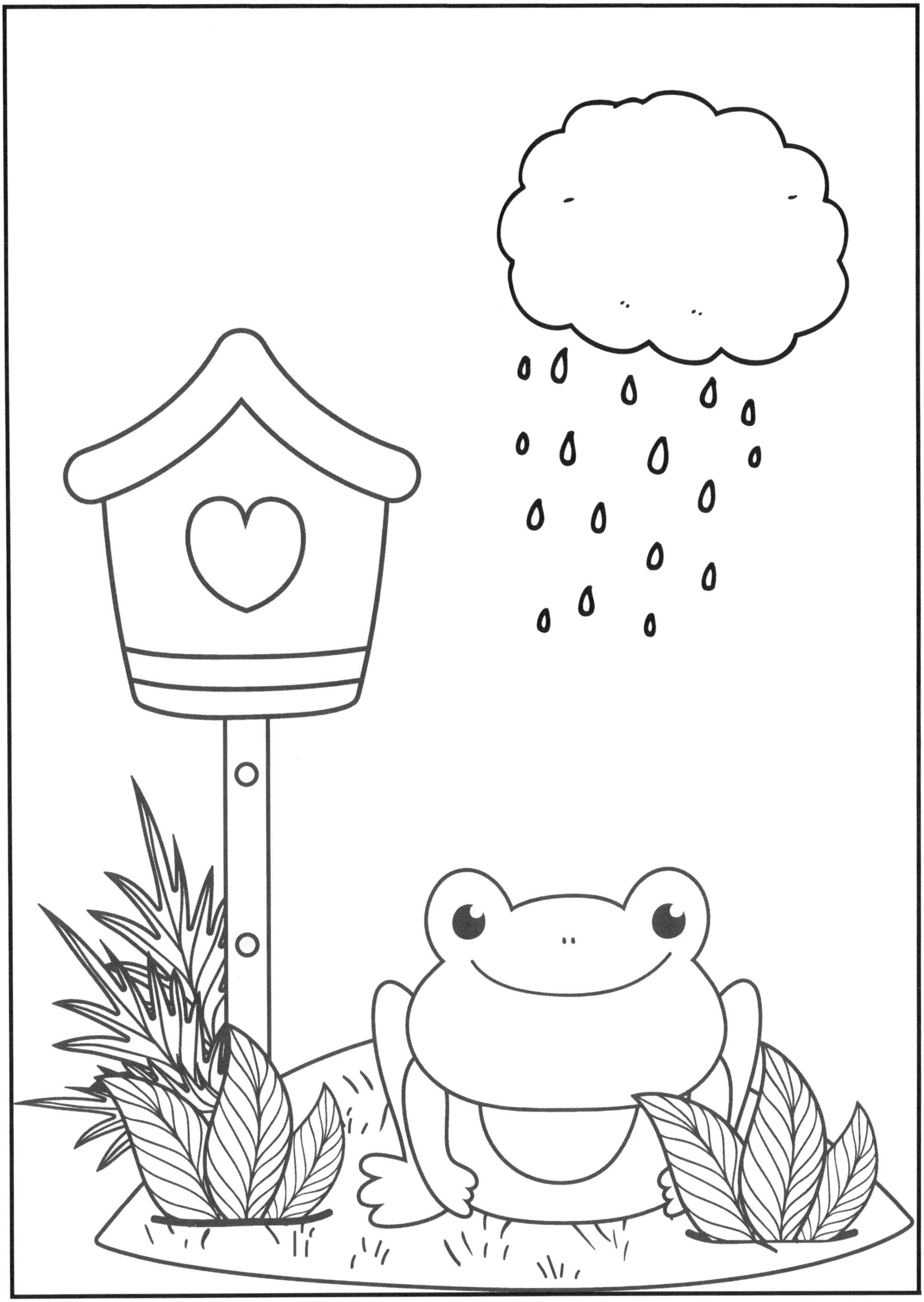

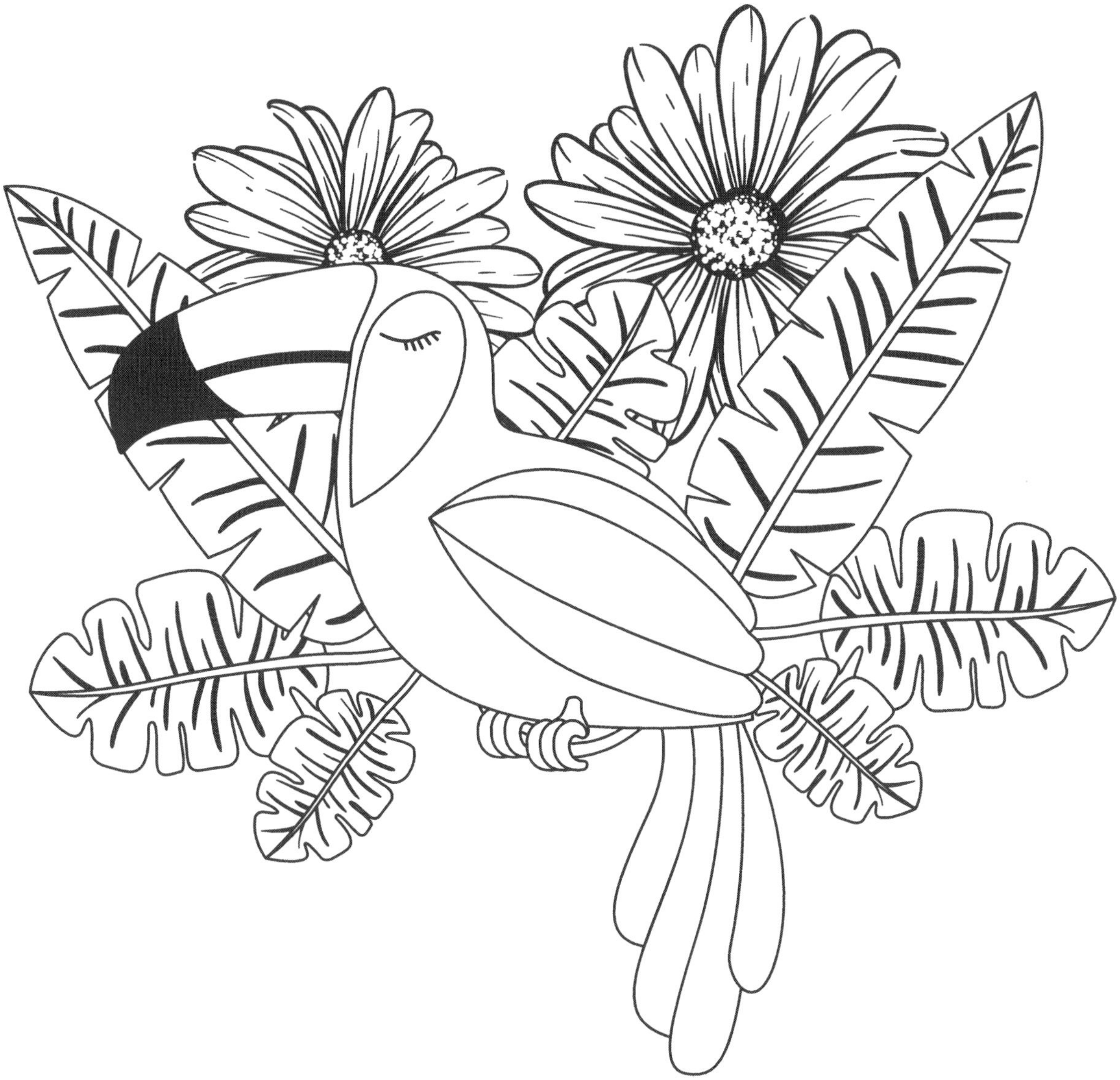

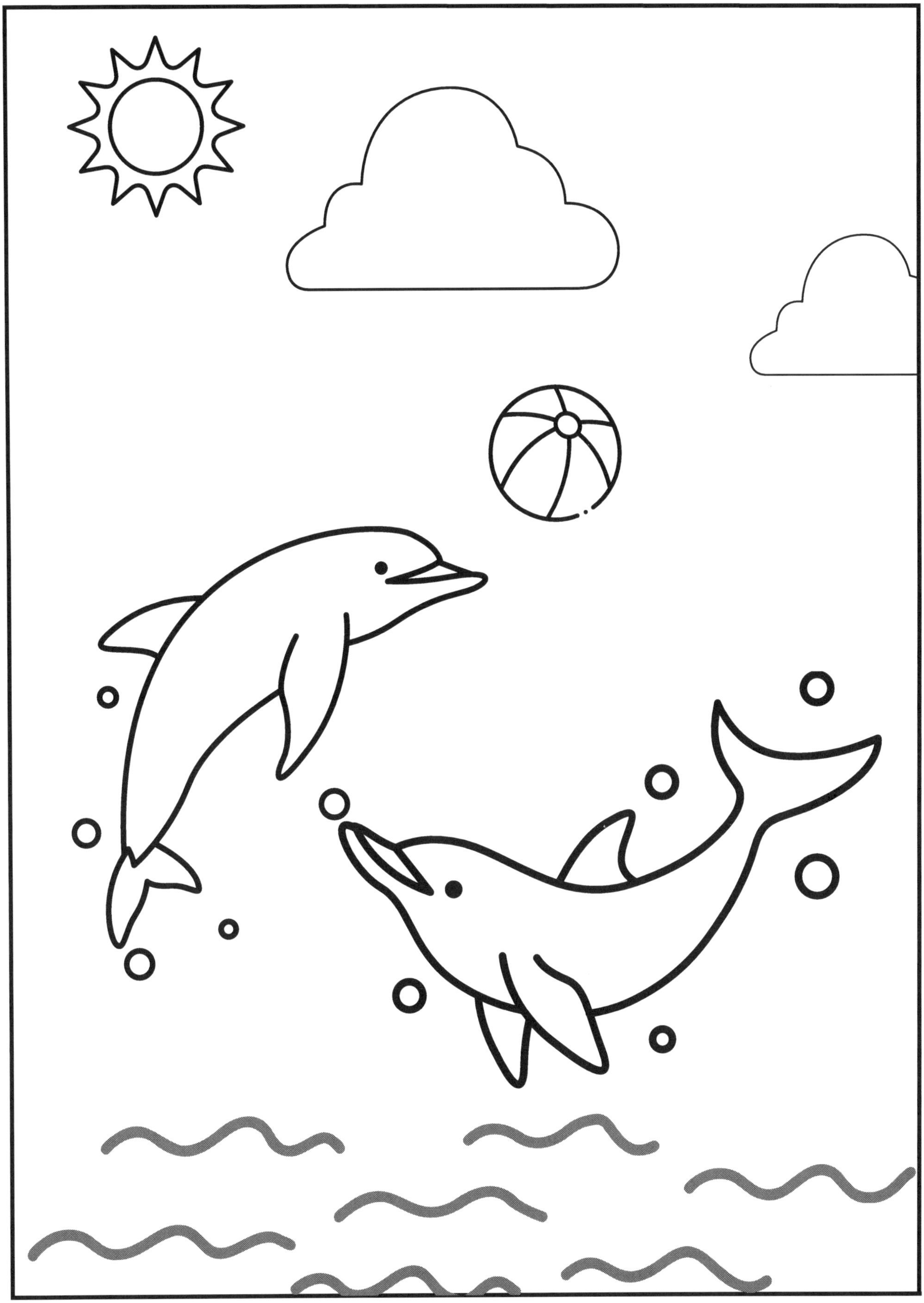

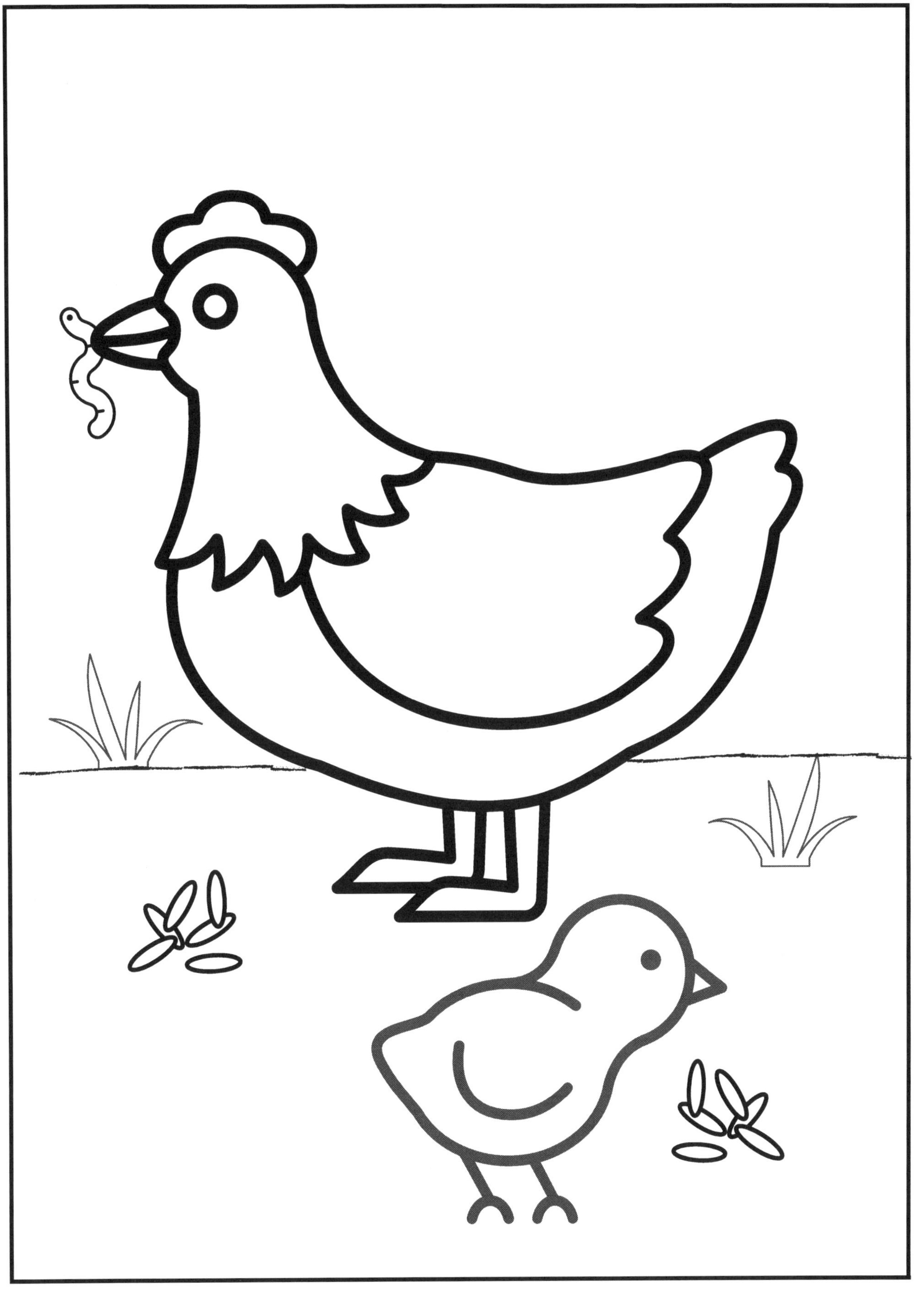

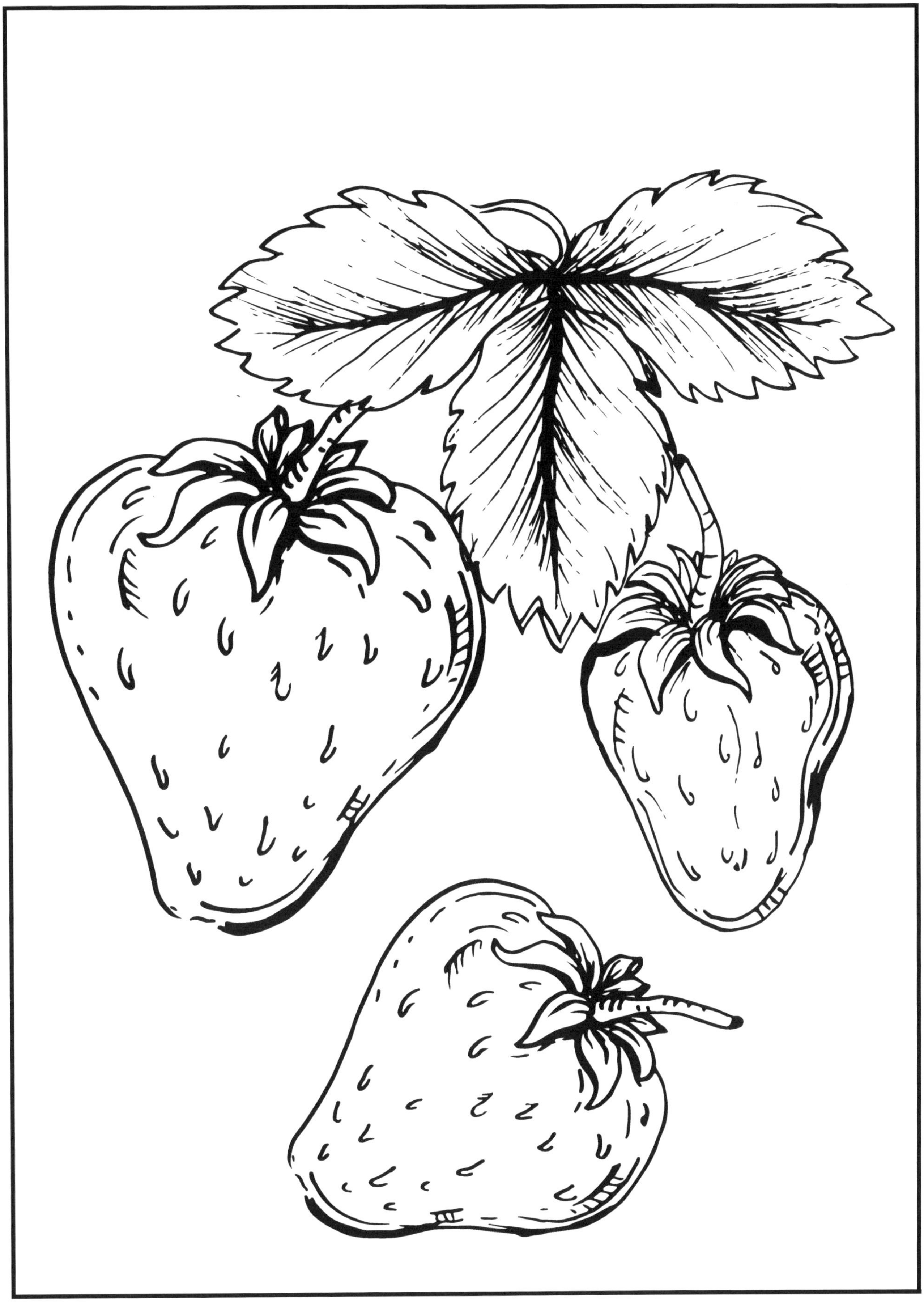

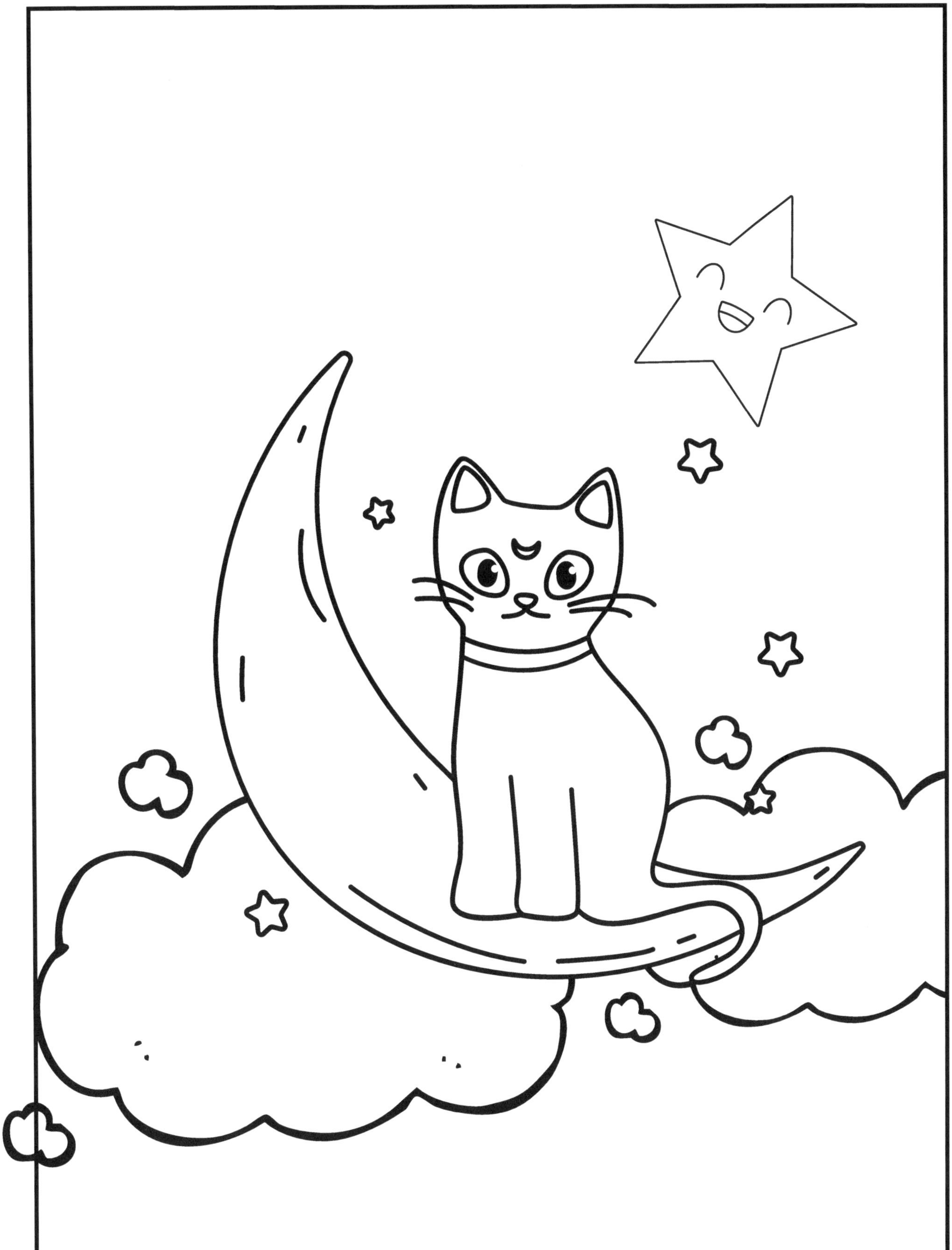

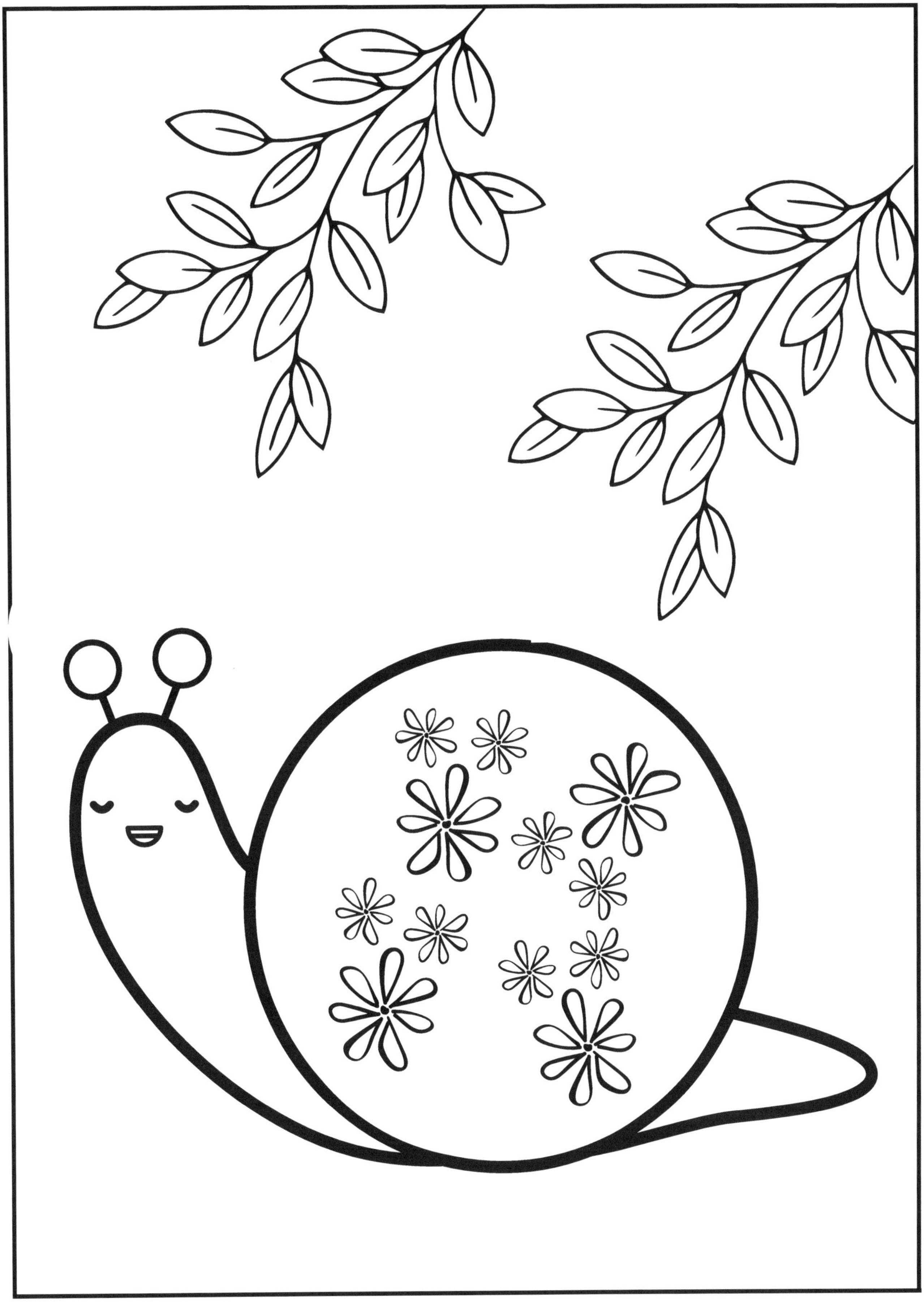

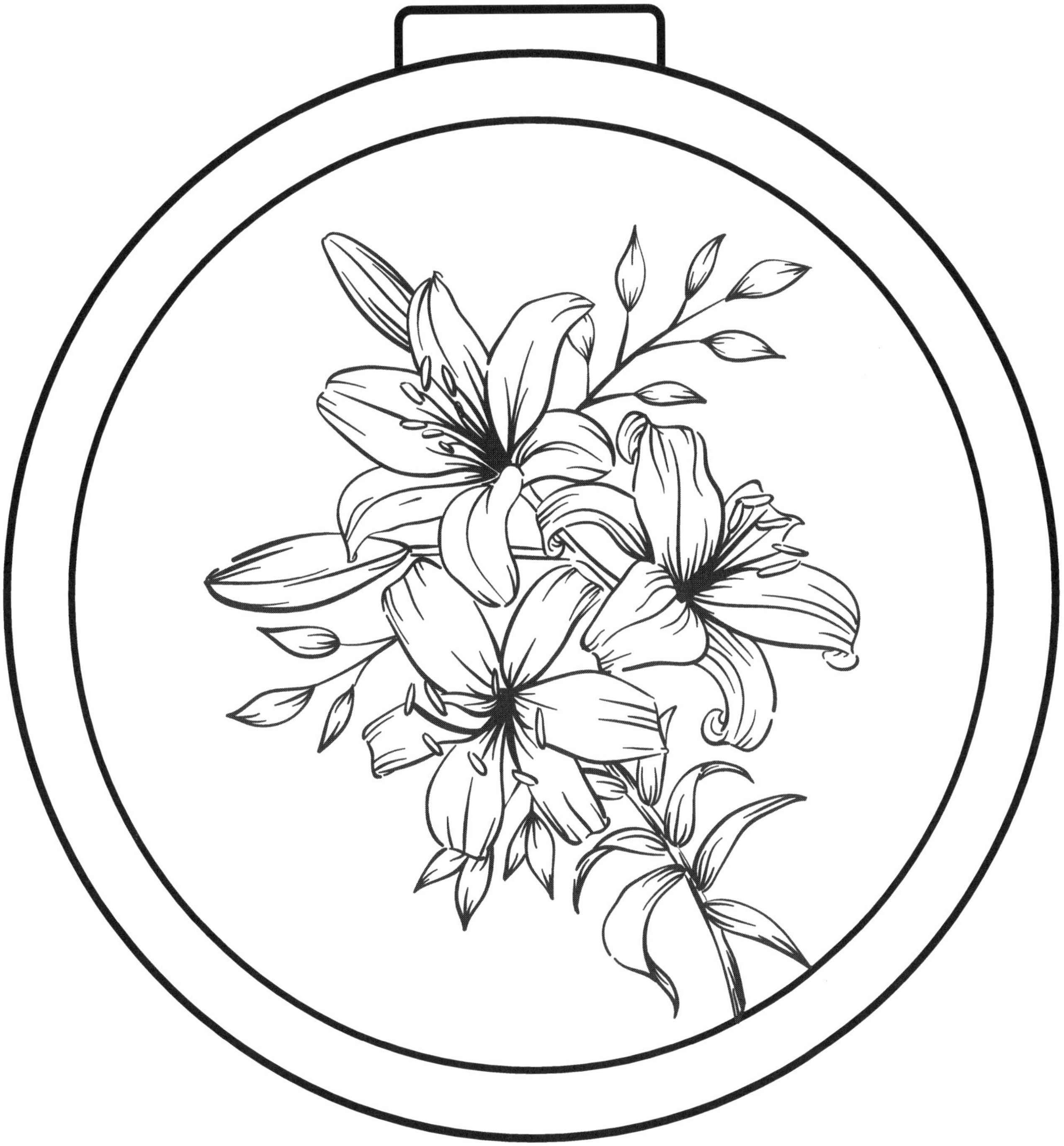

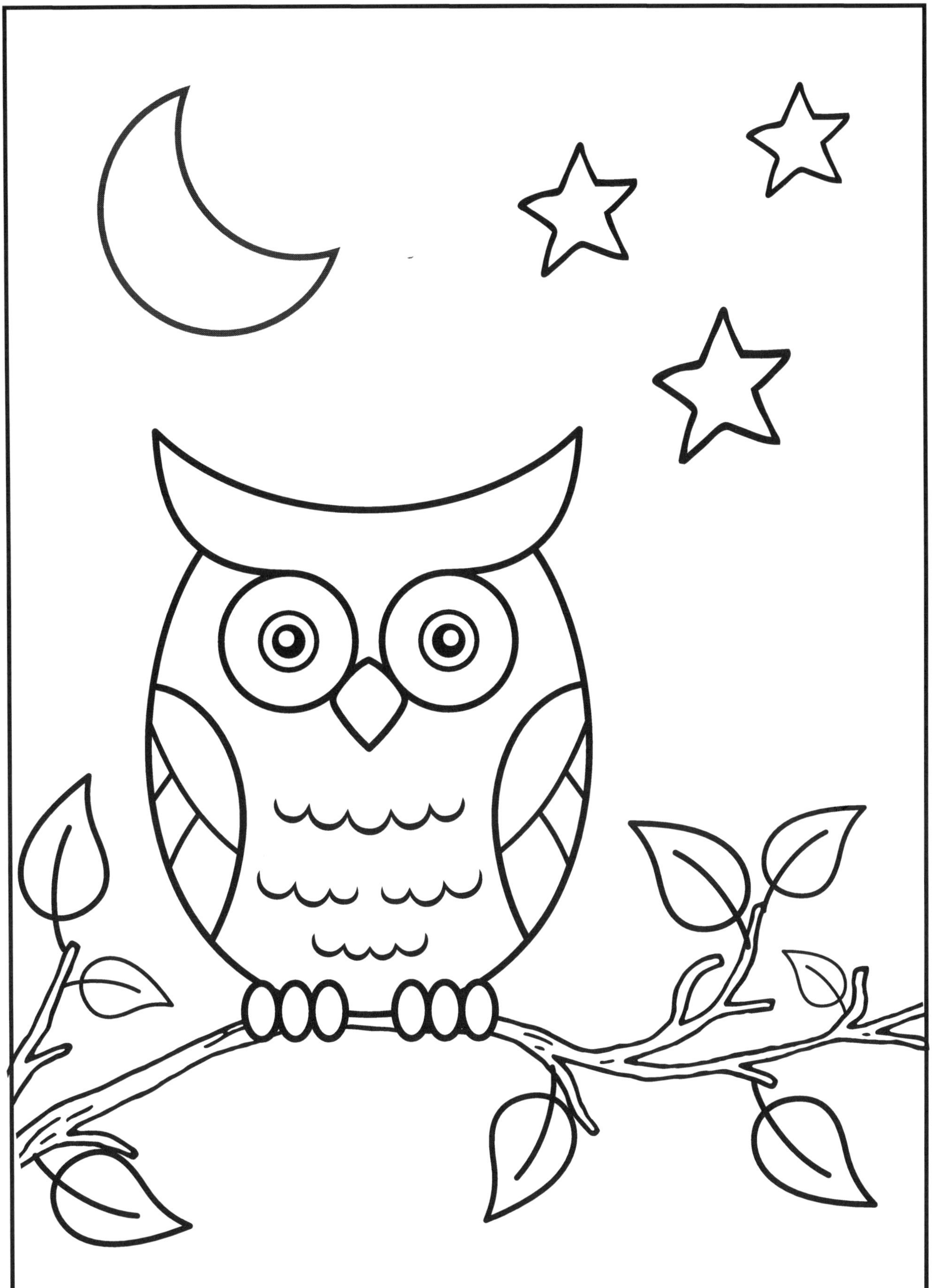

FRUITS

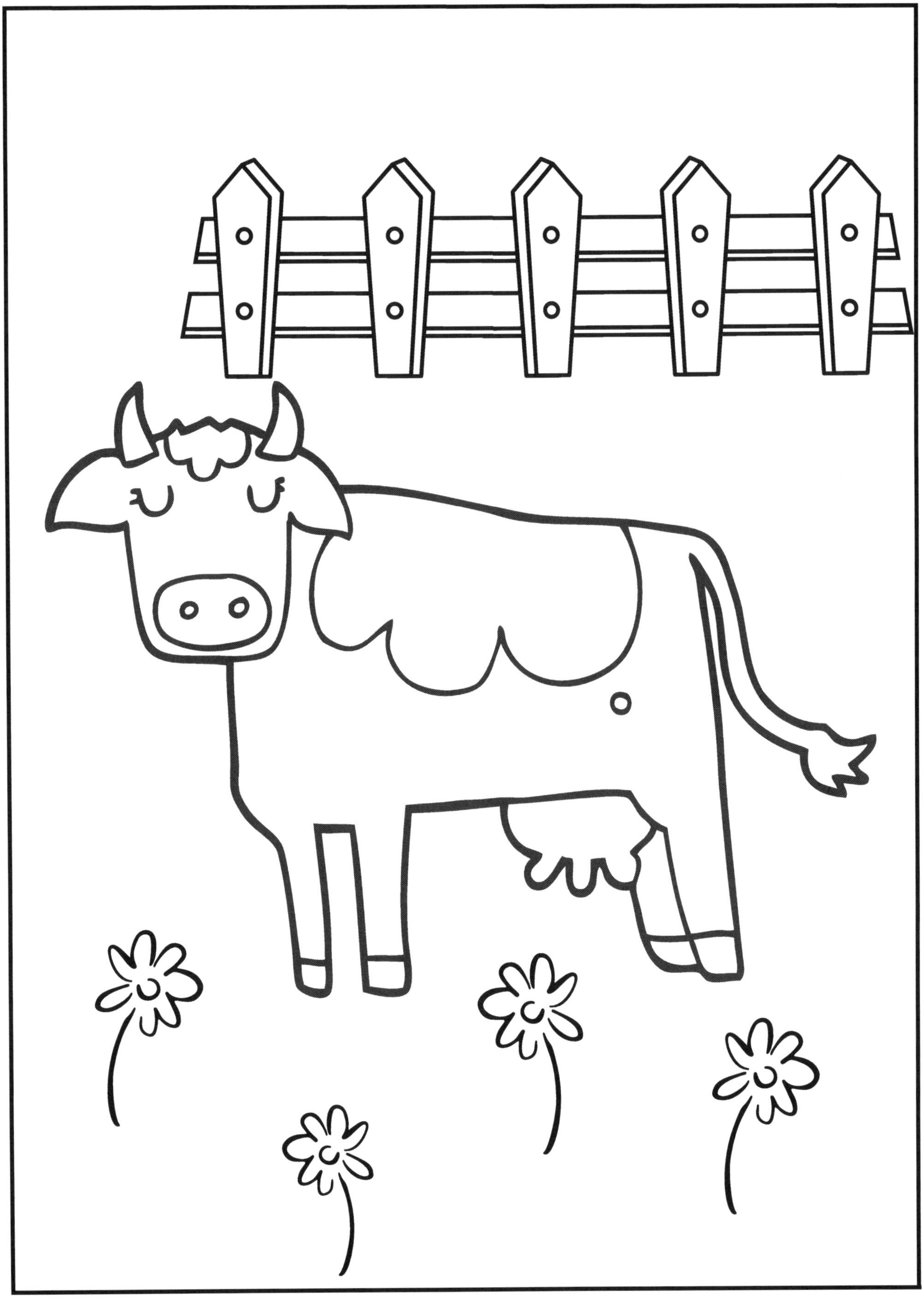

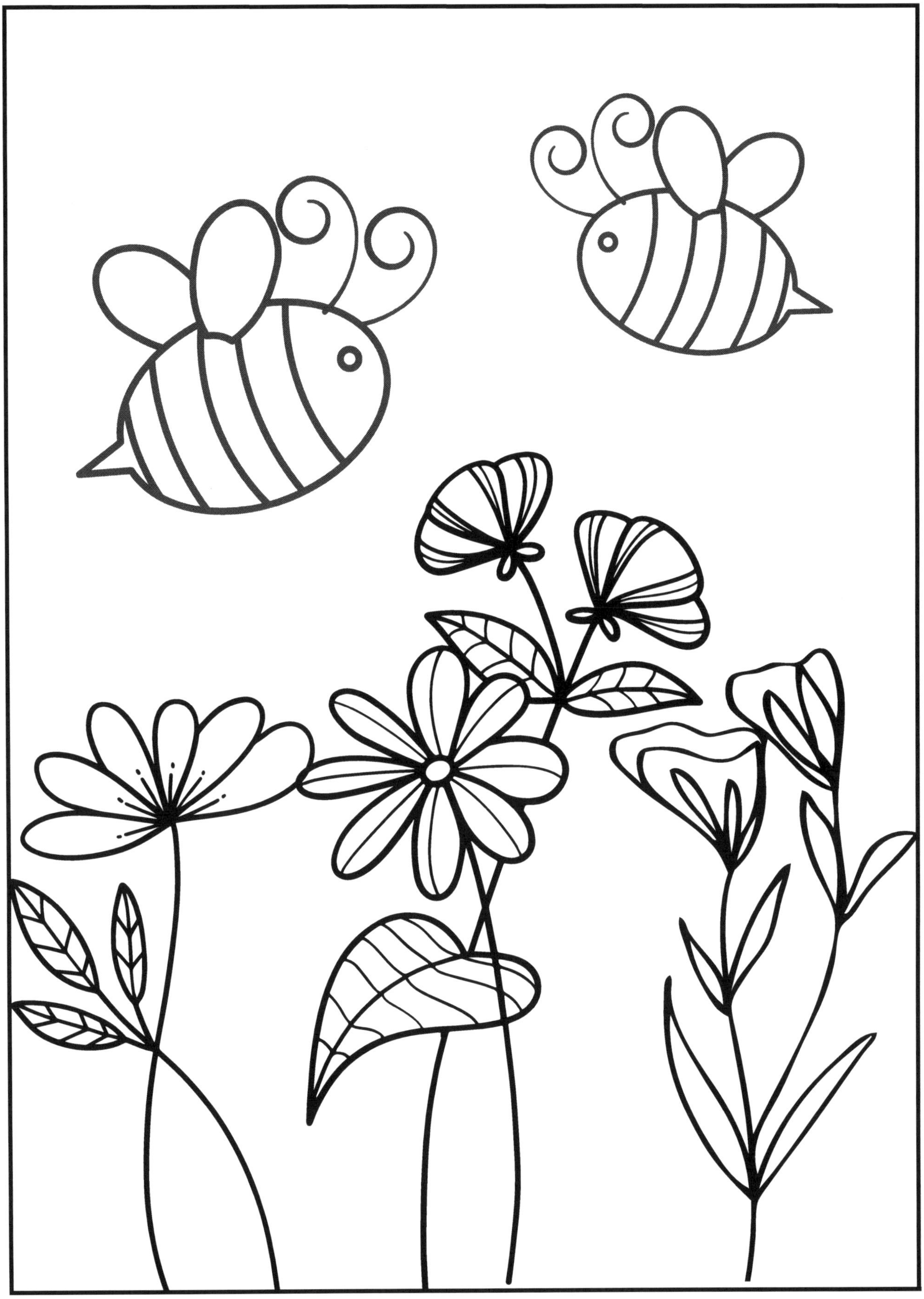

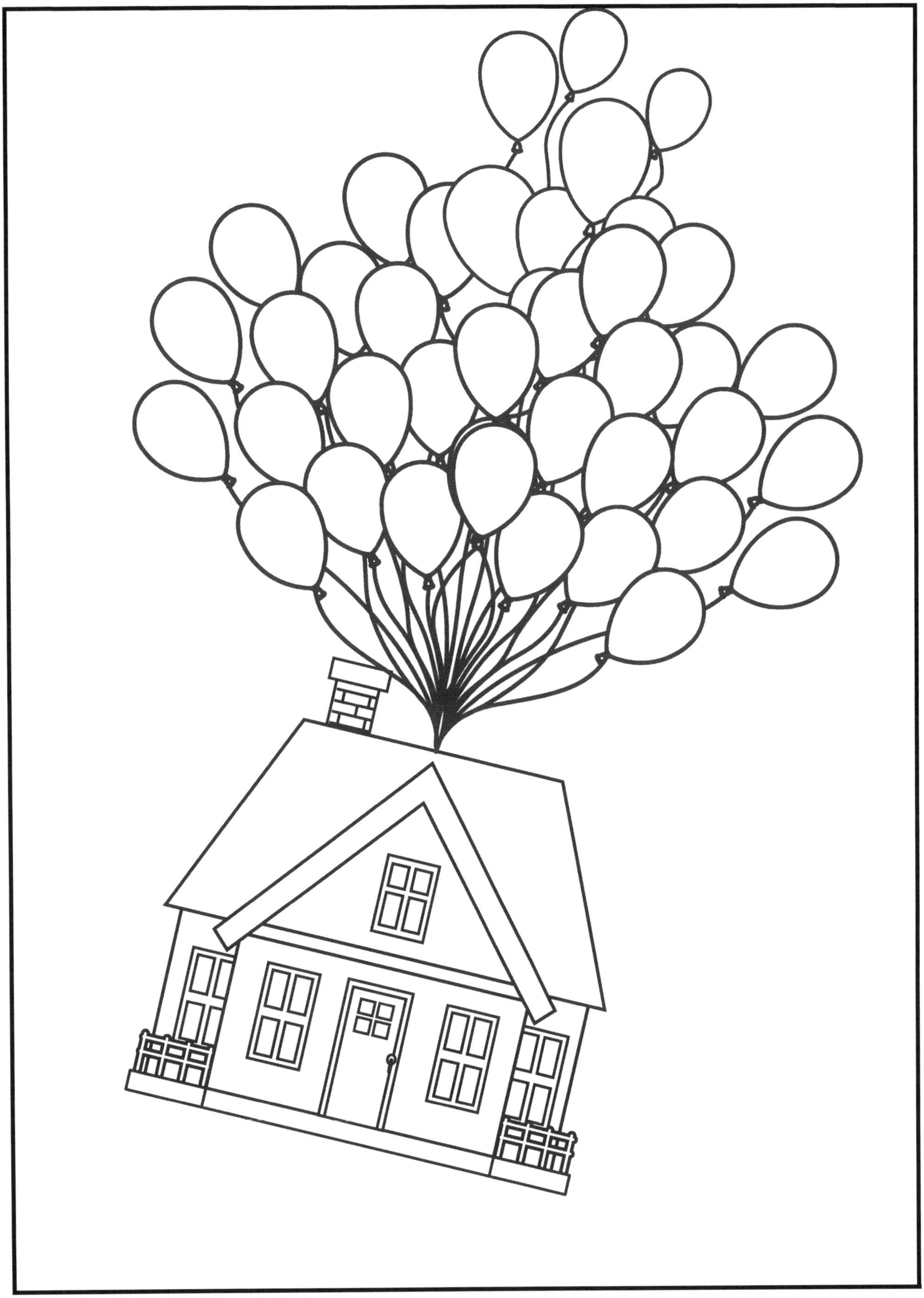

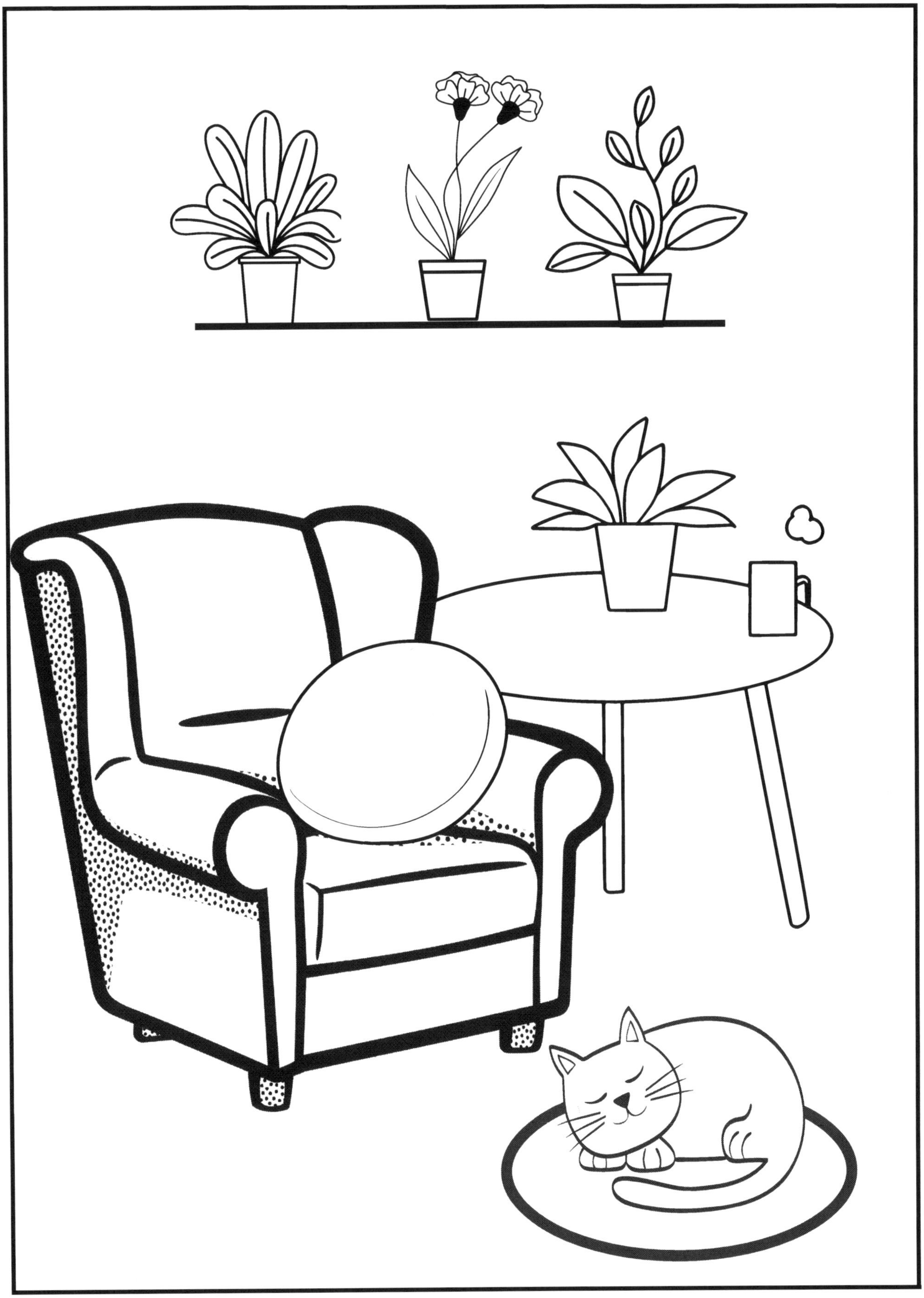

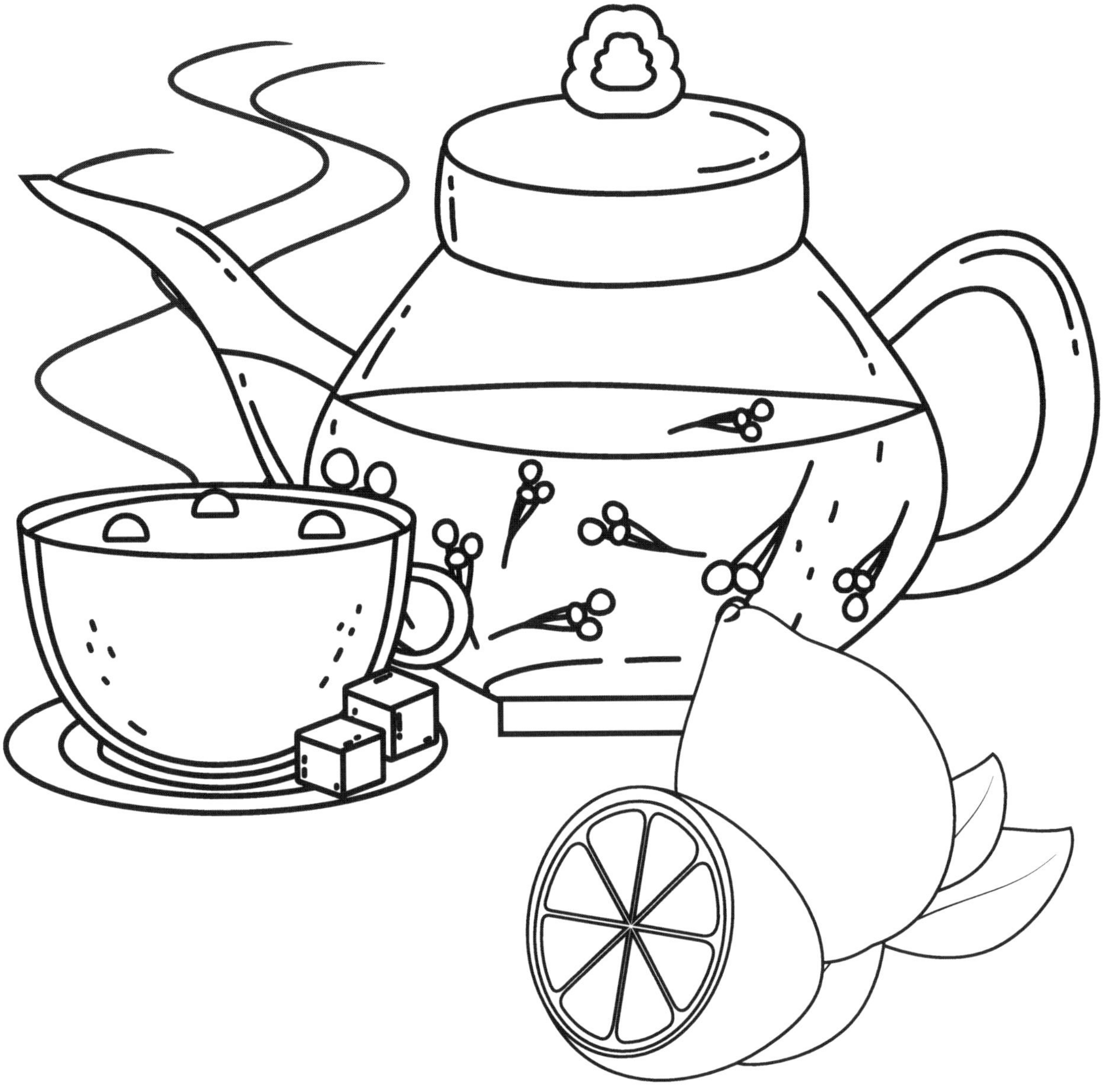

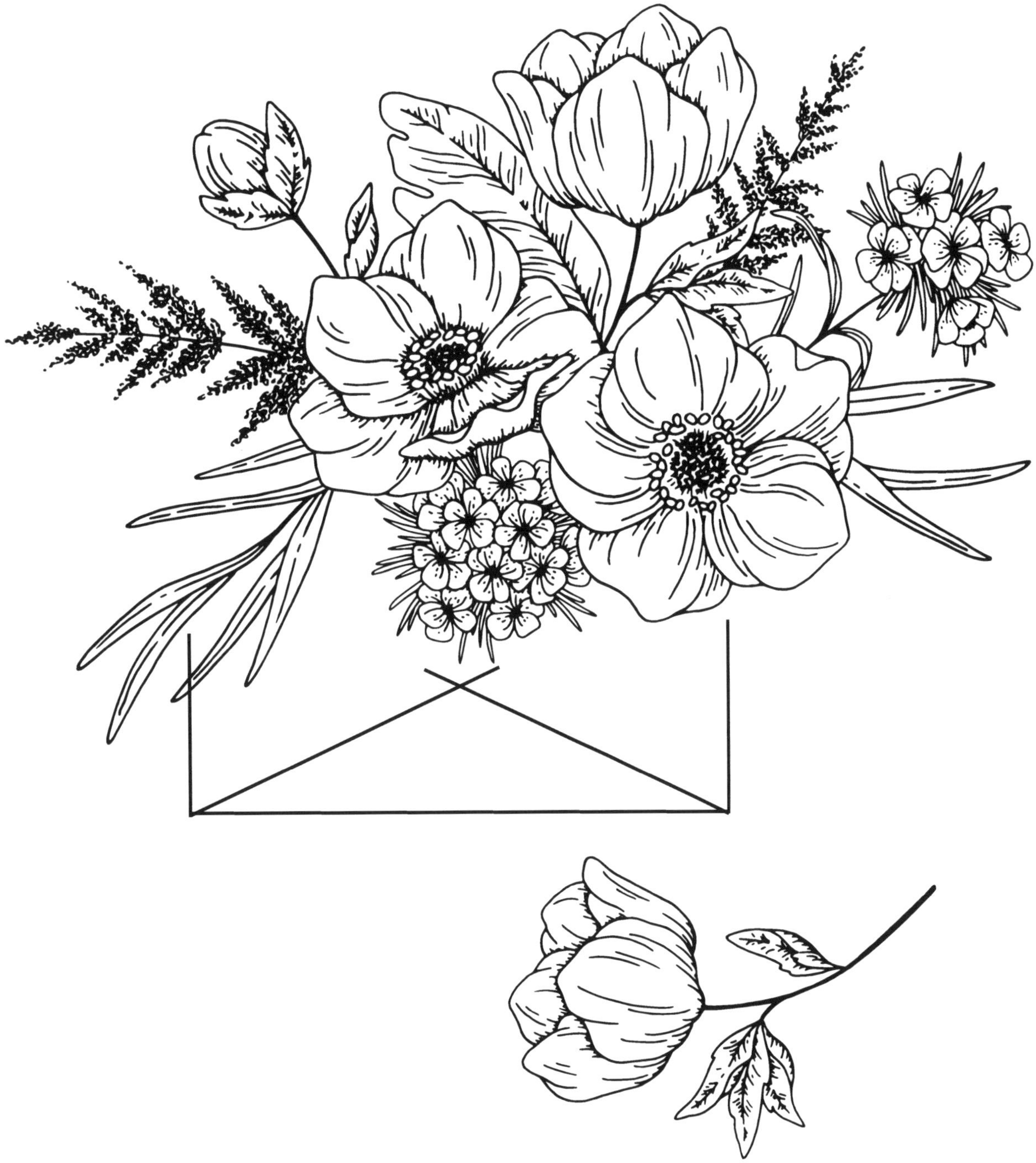

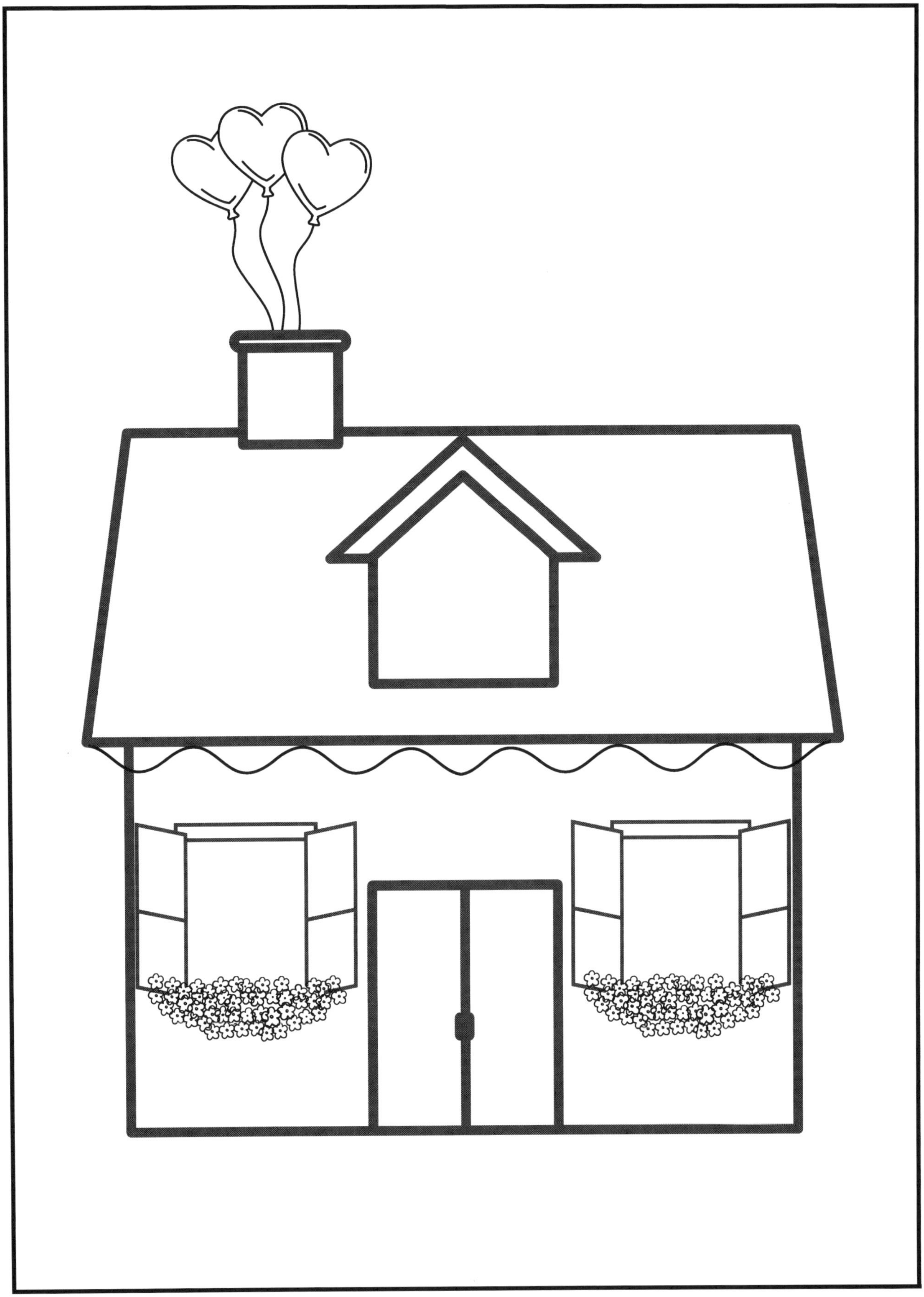

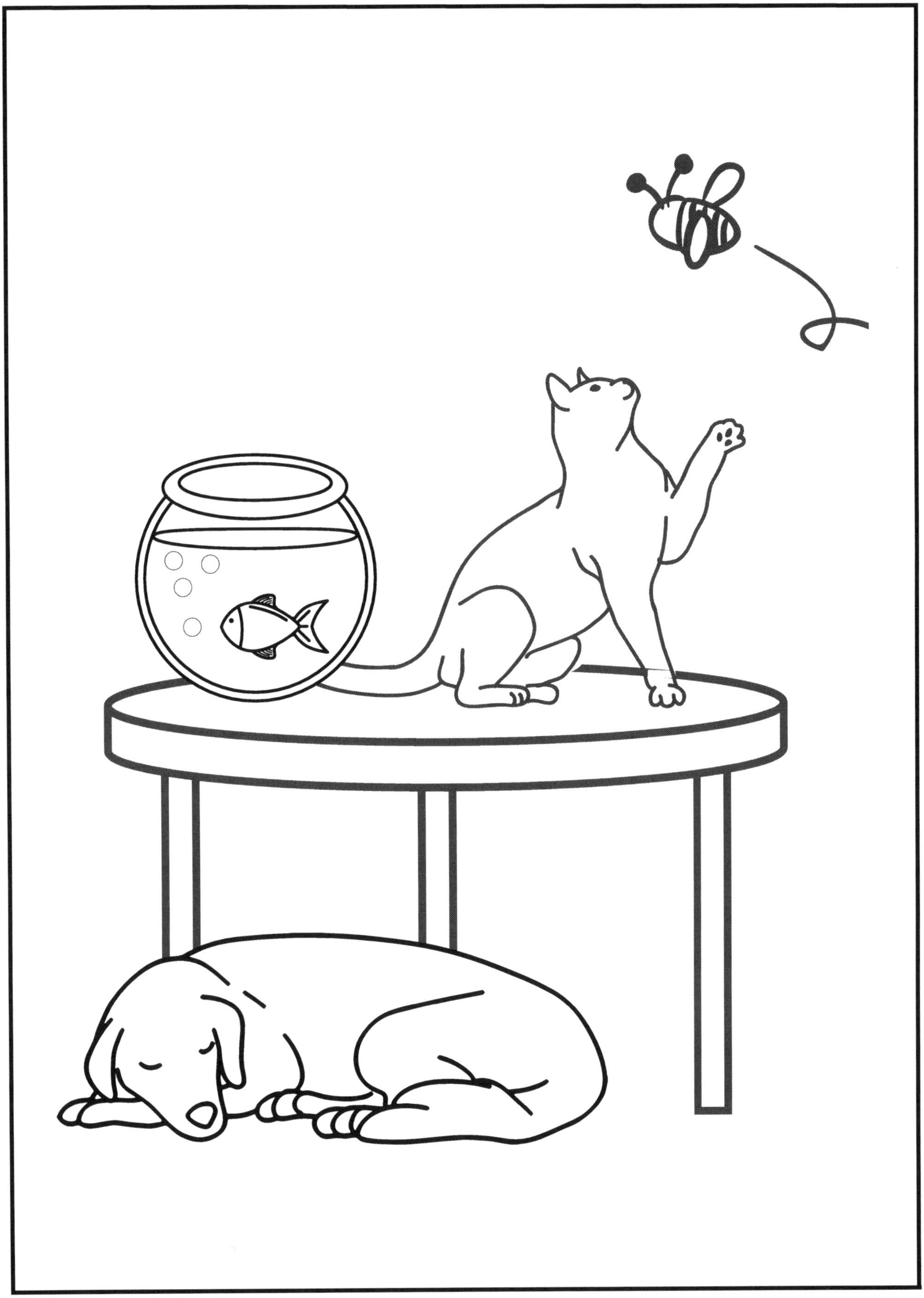

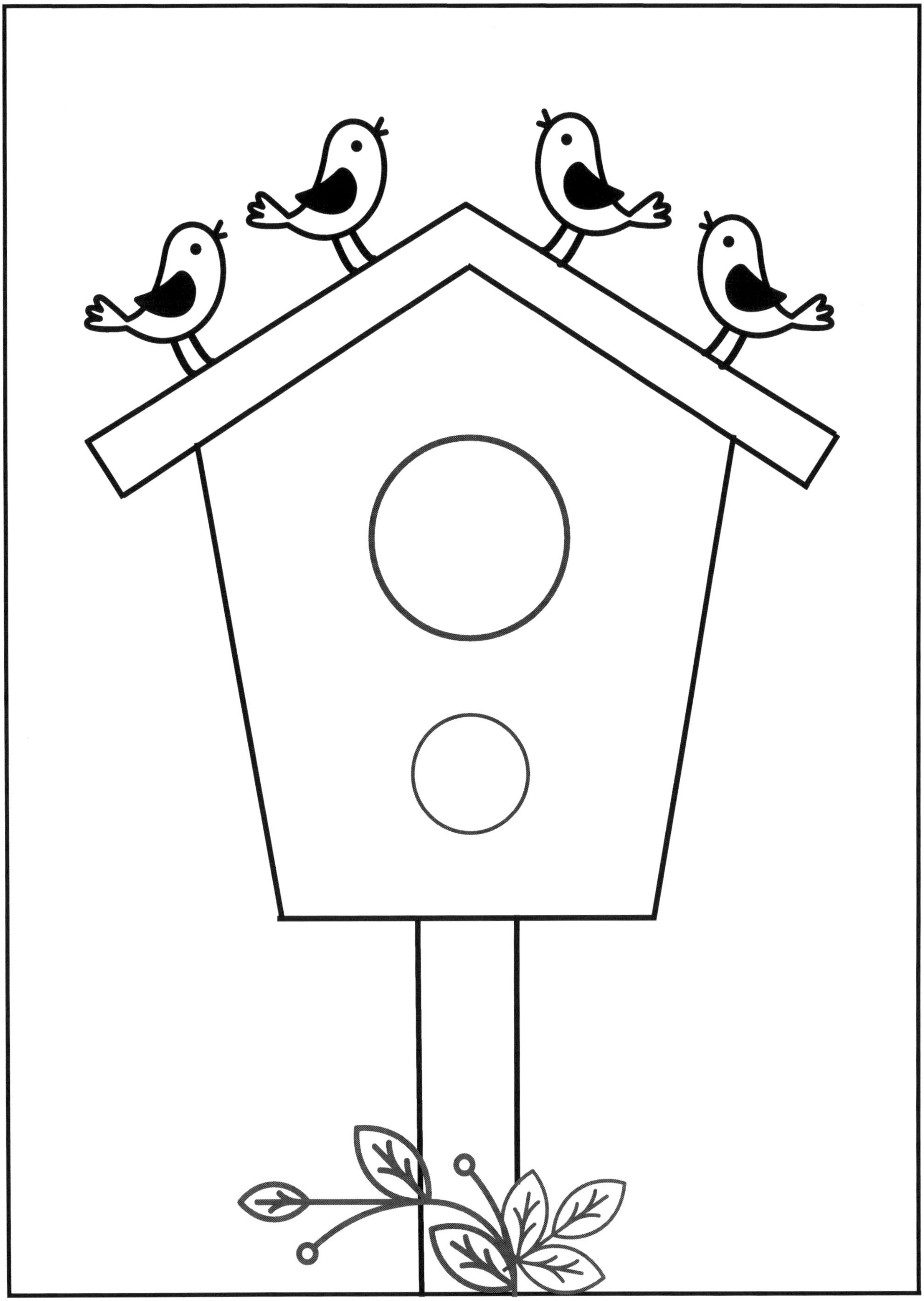

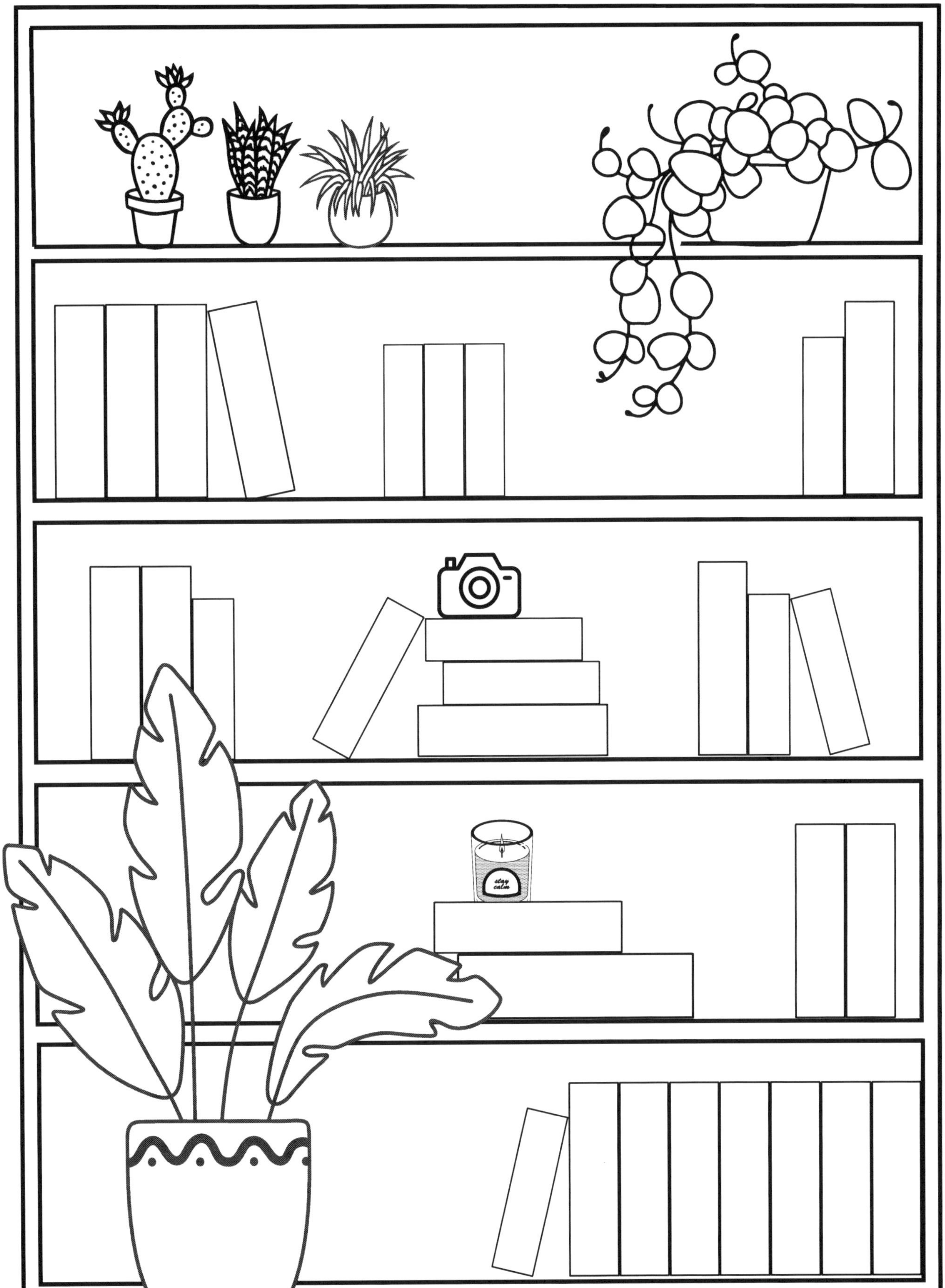
stay
calm

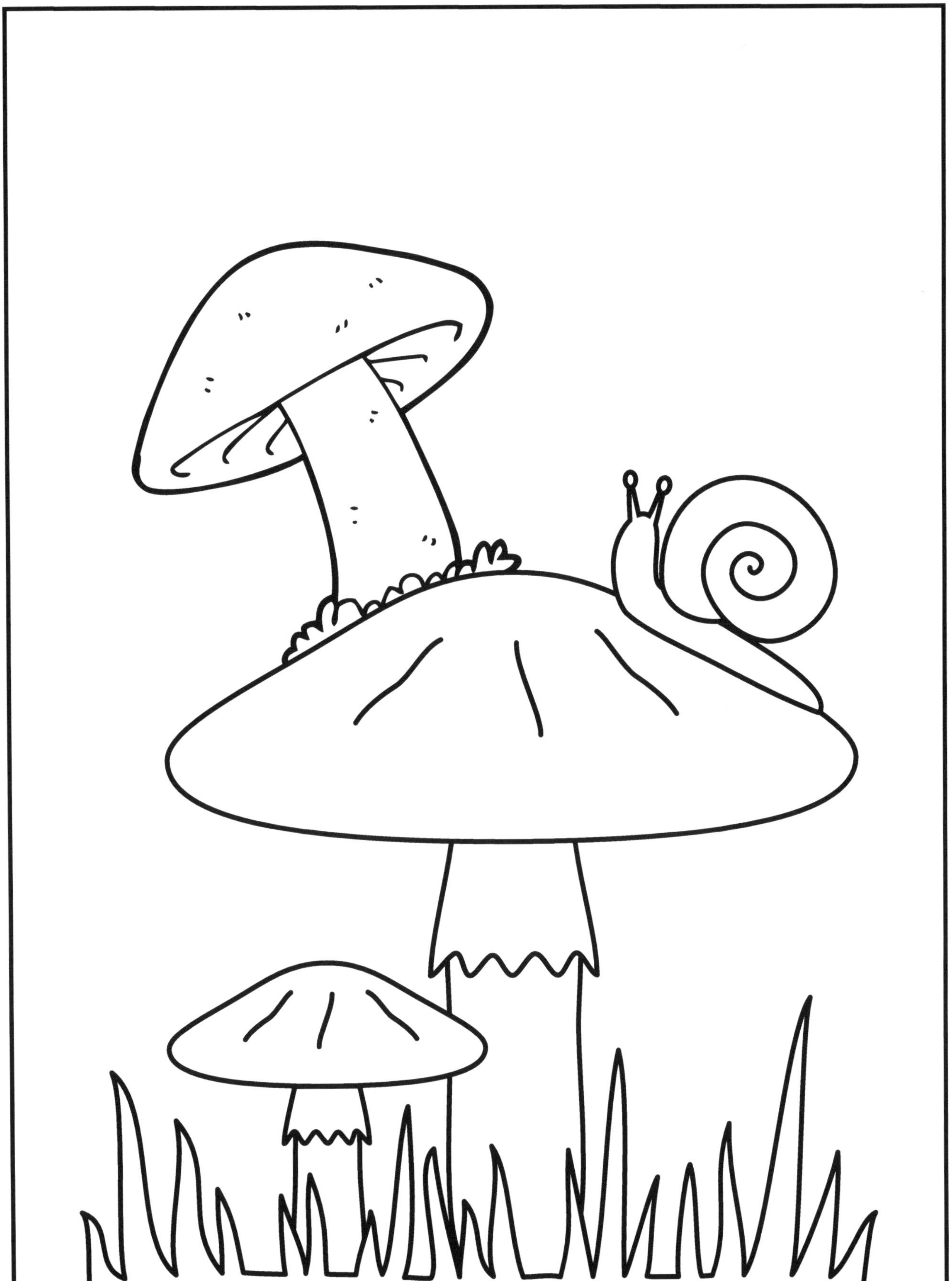

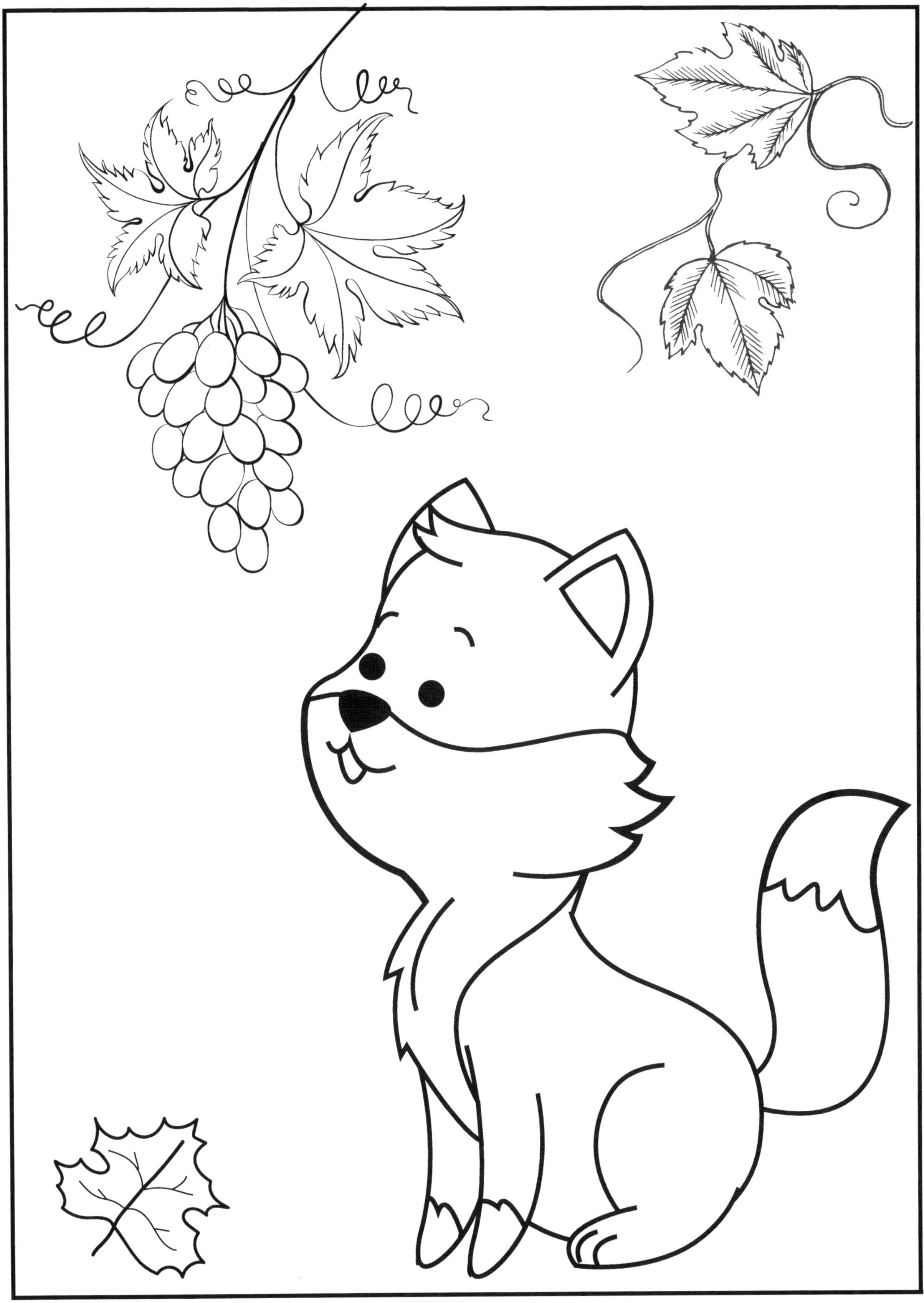

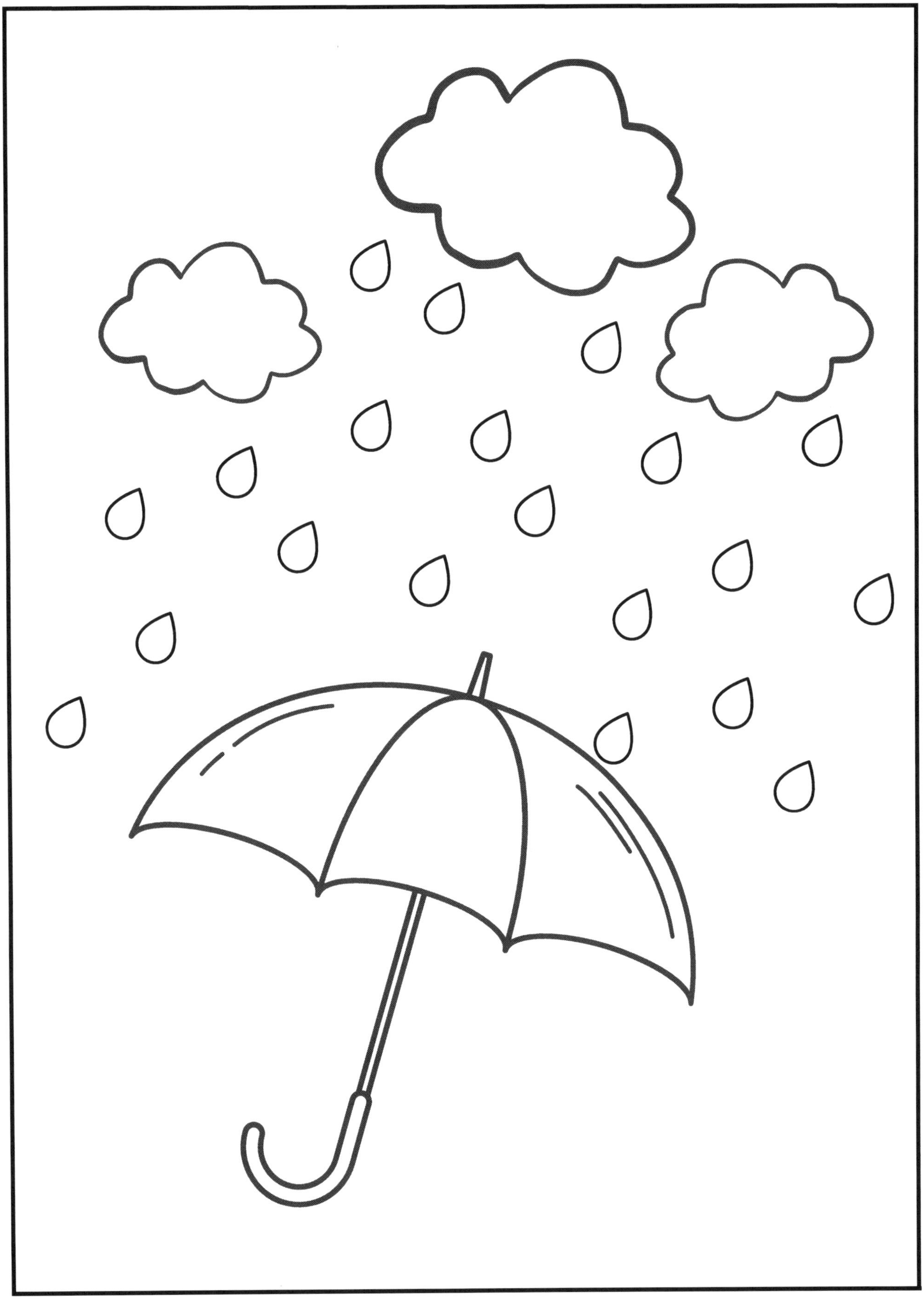

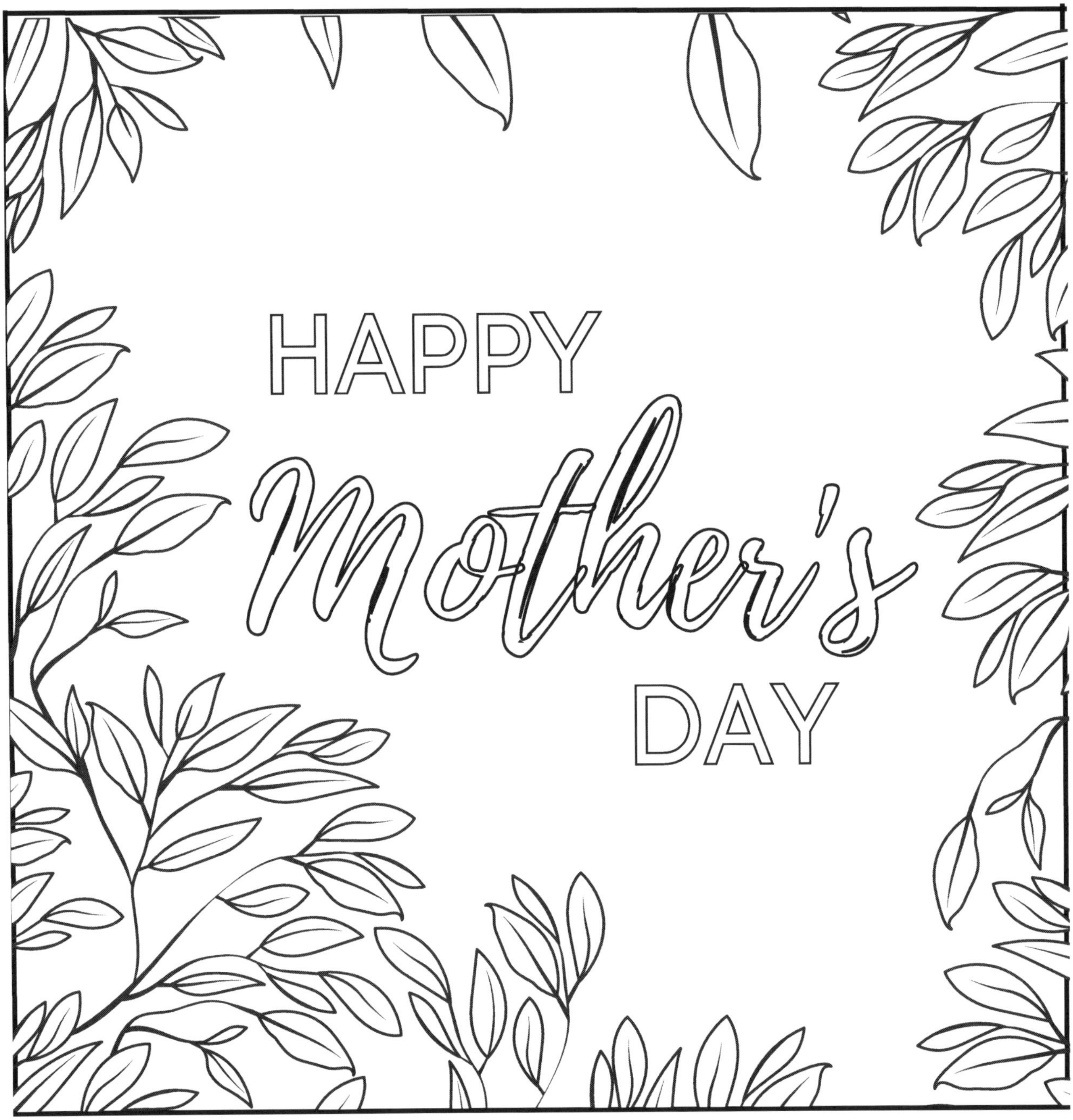
HAPPY
Mother's
DAY

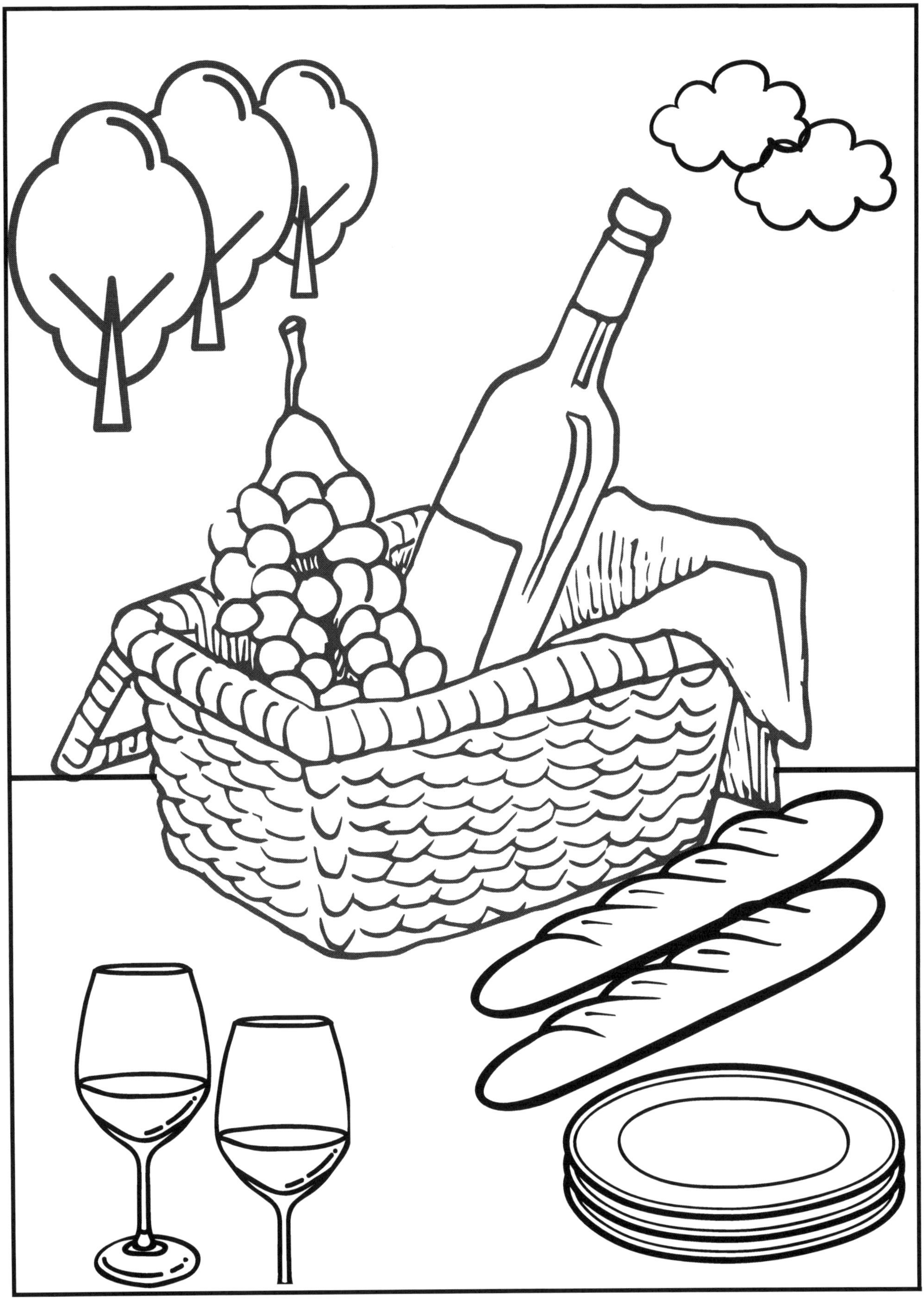

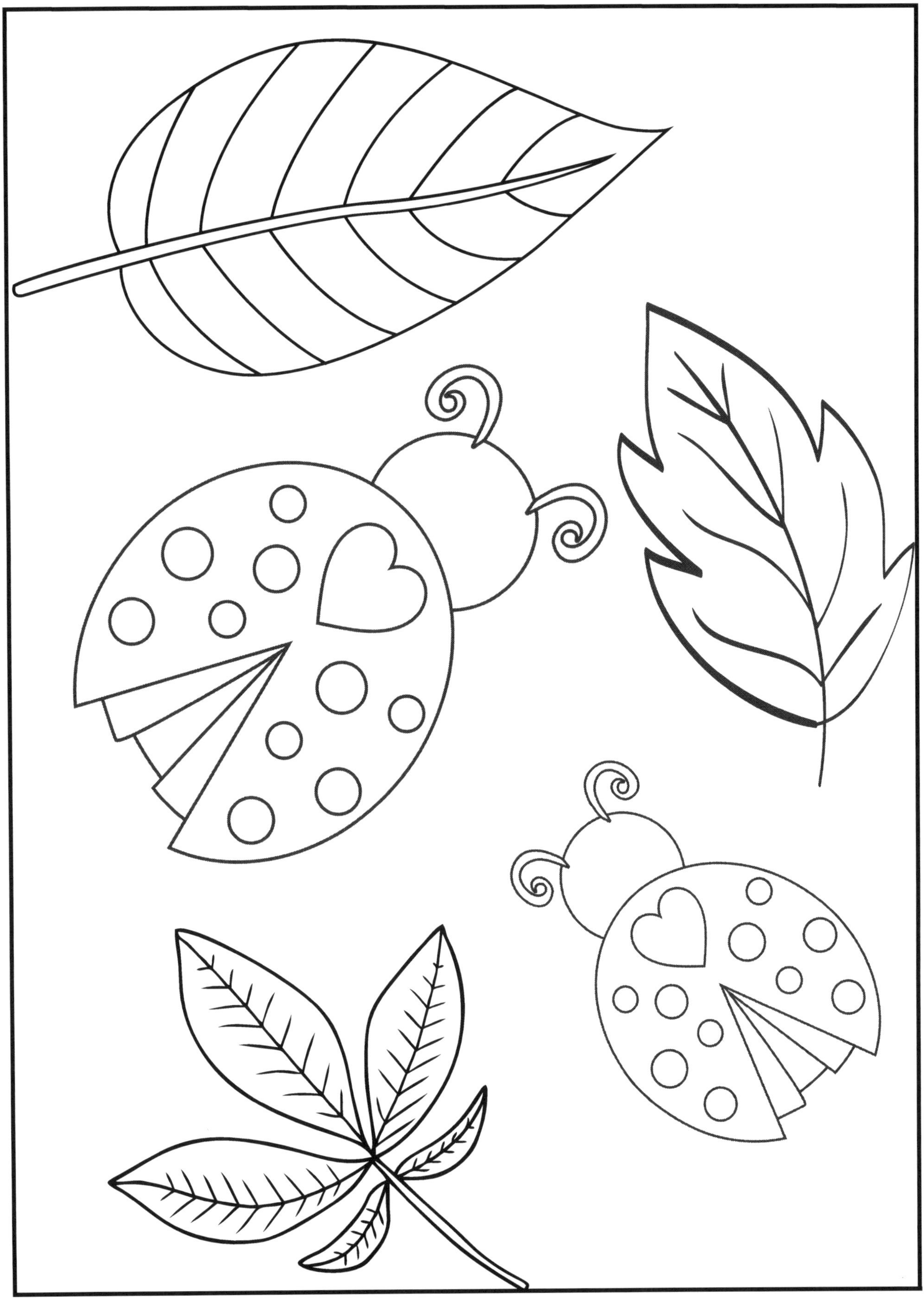

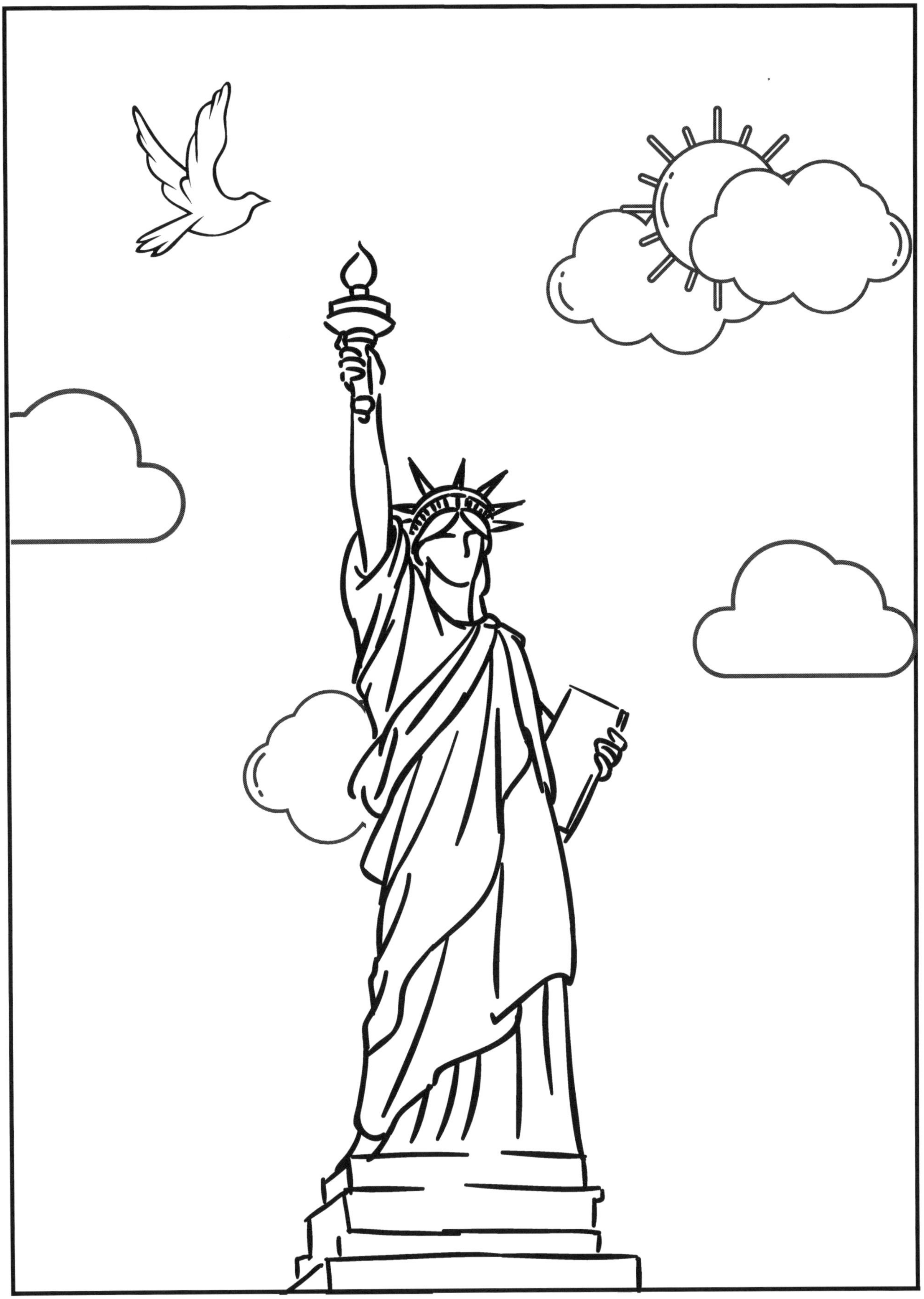

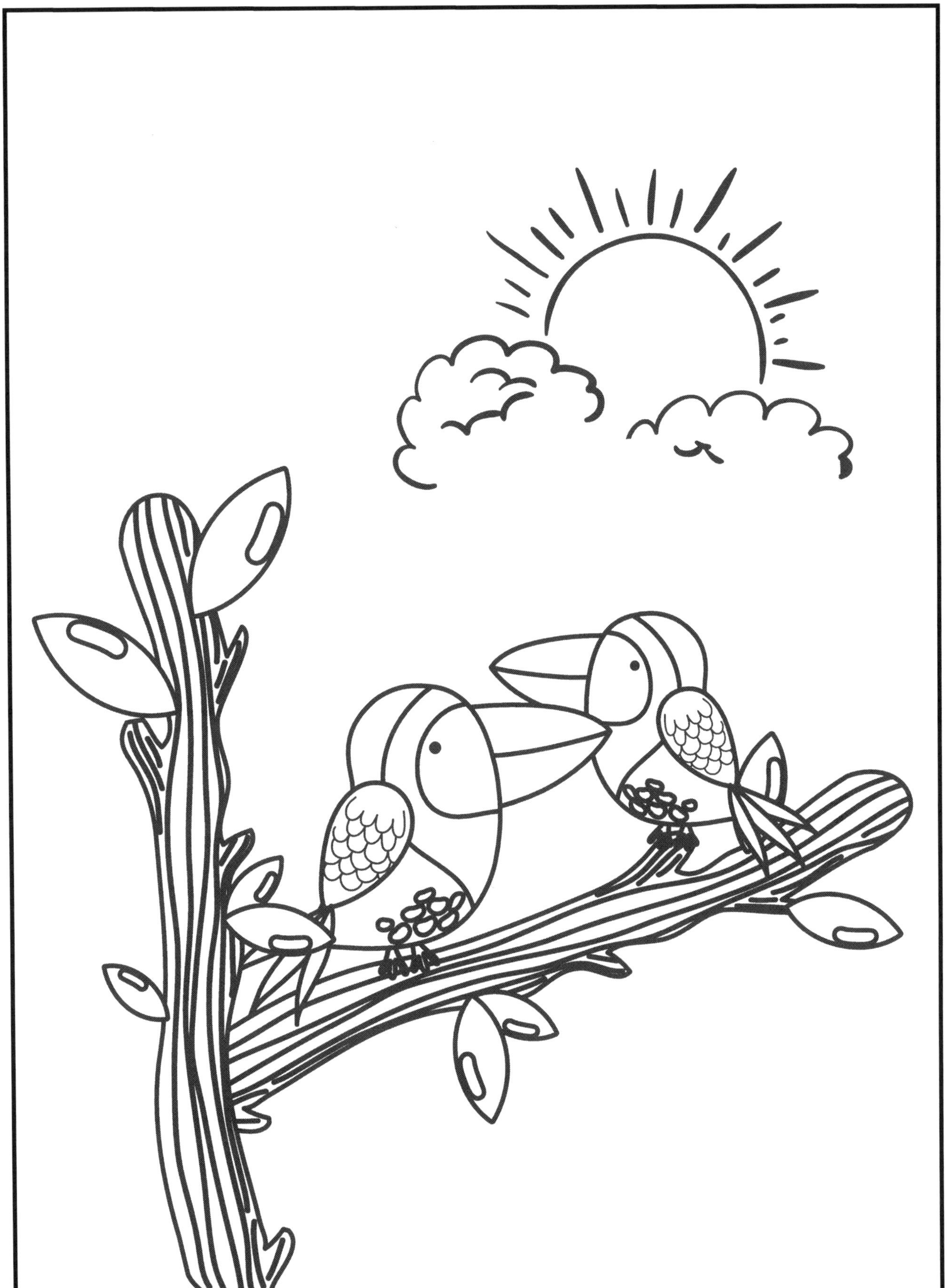

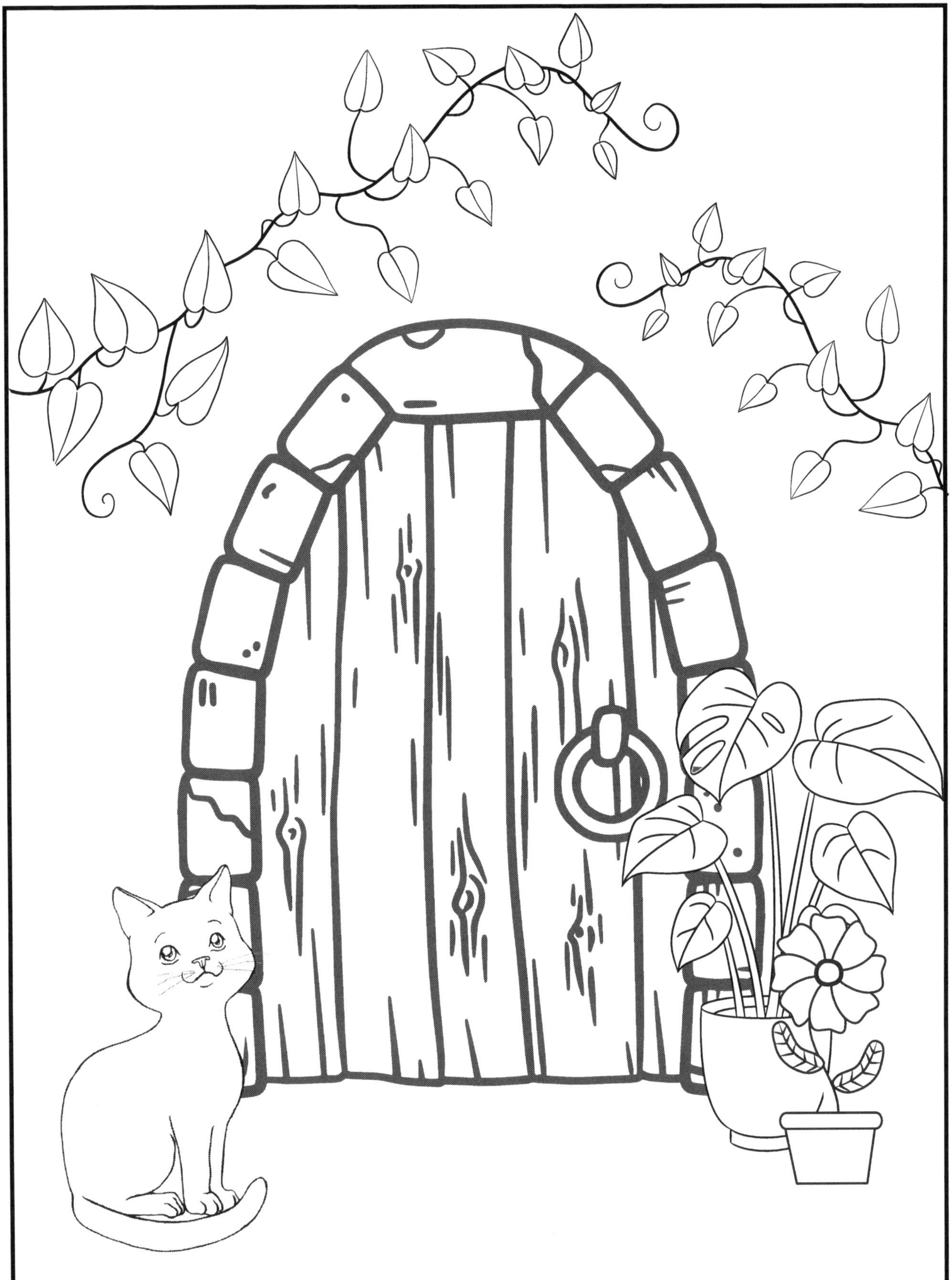

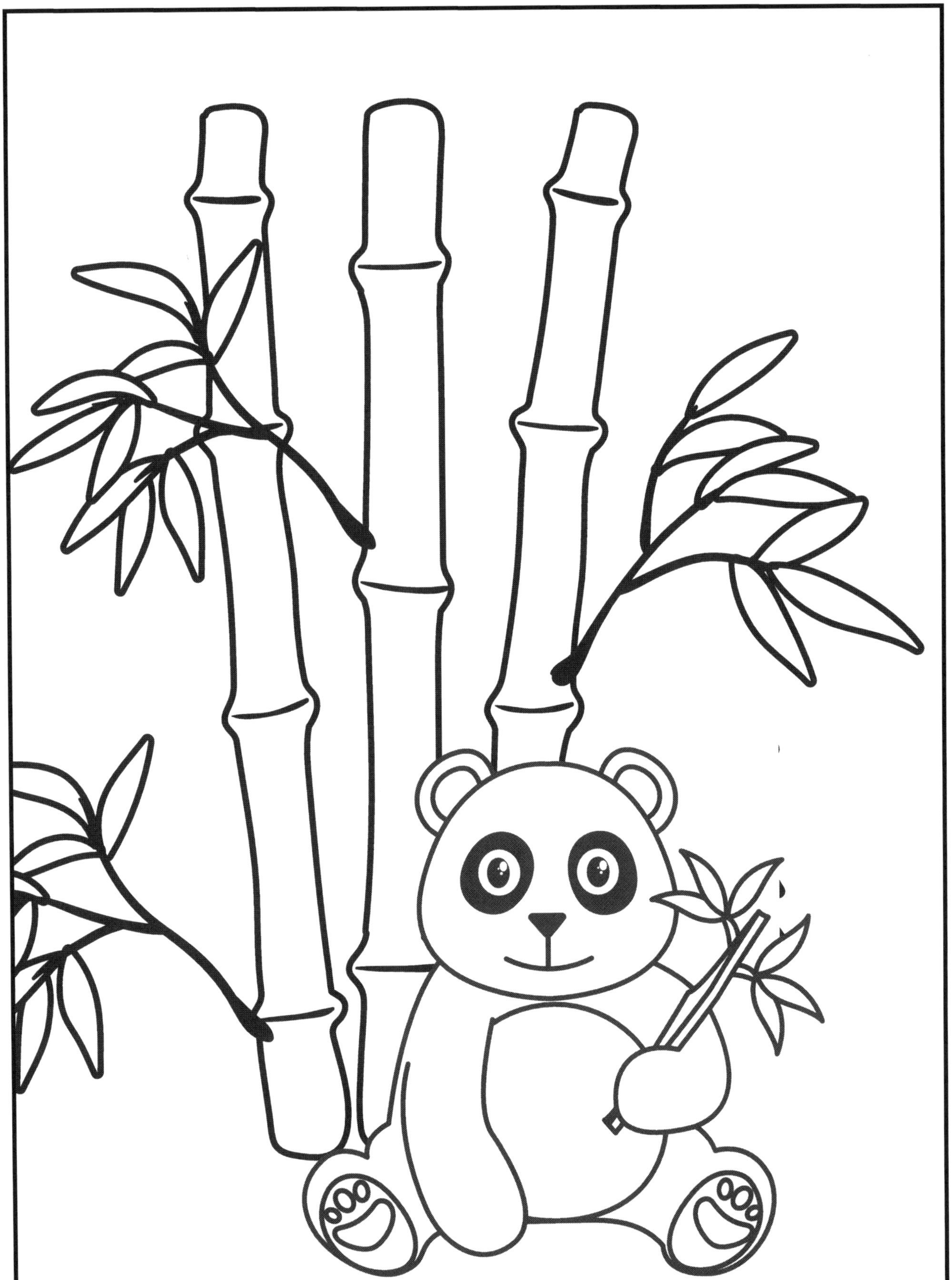

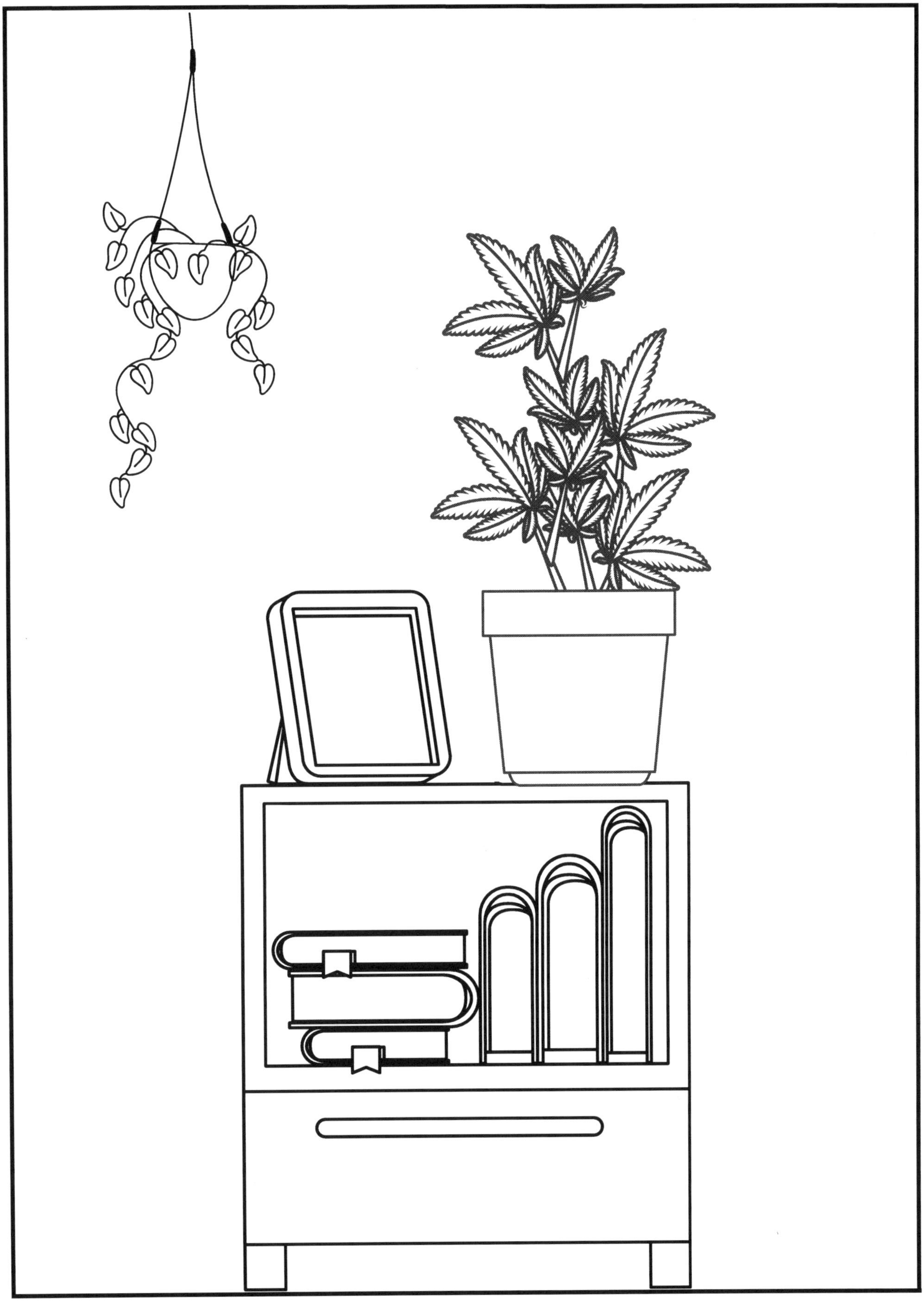

Made in United States
Orlando, FL
24 November 2024

54374956R00059